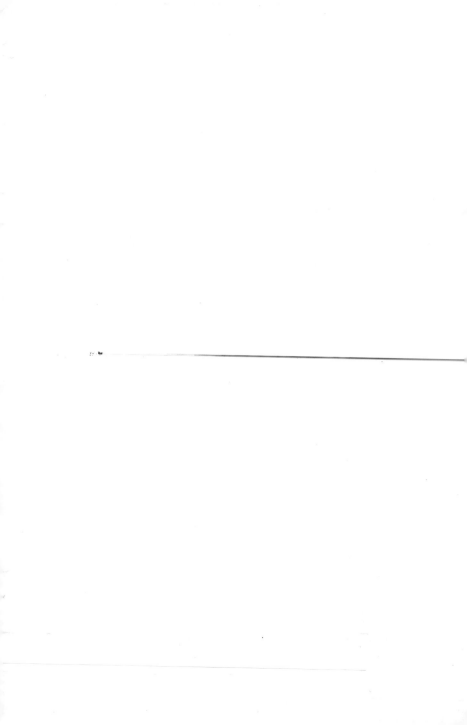

OPPORTUNITIES IN
MARKETING
CAREERS

Margery Steinberg

Foreword by
Philip Kotler
Northwestern University

VGM Career Horizons
A Division of National Textbook Company
4255 West Touhy Avenue
Lincolnwood, Illinois 60646-1975 U.S.A.

Cover Photo Credits:

Front cover: upper left, American Marketing
Association; upper right, Shepard Henkin;
lower left, Hewlett Packard; lower right, Bell
& Howell Education Group, Inc.
Back cover: upper left and lower right,
American Marketing Association; upper right,
General Motors Corporation; lower left,
Ruder Finn & Rotman.

ABOUT THE AUTHOR

Margery Steinberg received her Ph.D. from the University of Connecticut and is currently a full-time faculty member at the University of Hartford, where she teaches marketing and advertising at both the graduate and undergraduate levels. Active in the American Marketing Association, Steinberg holds the office of Divisional Vice-President for Collegiate Activities. Involved in the regional business scene through participation in several professional organizations and committees, Steinberg also lends her marketing expertise to many prominent local and national businesses as a consultant.

ACKNOWLEDGMENTS

Writing a book is not an easy task. Many minds and experiences contribute to an author's knowledge of the subject matter and understanding of the readers' needs and interests.

I hereby acknowledge those who contributed to this author's endeavor in writing this book: the staff and membership of the American Marketing Association who have enabled me to experience and practice marketing in its purest form, my fellow board members with whom I have worked so closely in enhancing the growth and professionalism, and particularly the Collegiate Activities Council members and collegiate chapters with whom I have worked for the past six years to create educational opportunities for students in the field of marketing; my colleagues at the University of Hartford who have both challenged and supported me; my students who have given me direction for my work through their curiosity about the field and their career interests; my research assistants Linda

Plank and Amy Alperi who spent tireless hours in the library researching the most current and informative materials for this book; and our department secretary, Joanne Burke, who pulled together the loose ends.

FOREWORD

Among the many careers in business—accounting, finance, manufacturing, purchasing, personnel, and so on—marketing is one of the most exciting and rewarding. "There is never a dull moment" applies to this field. Talk to people in sales, advertising, product planning, sales promotion, and marketing research, and they will tell you that each day brings new challenges and calls for new solutions.

Marketing people get involved in one of two tasks. One task is to identify unsatisfied consumer needs and wants that might provide promising new business opportunities. Thus the Ford marketing people discovered some years ago that many young people would like to buy an affordable sports car—and they launched the Mustang. Identifying new opportunities involves market researchers, product developers, pricing experts, and market planners.

The second task is to attract new customers to existing products, services, and brands. This calls for identifying the groups of people who would benefit most from an offer, preparing advertising to communicate the offer's benefits, making sales calls on prospects, designing sales promotions to stimulate purchase, negotiating, and several other skills.

Marketing is not only a challenge to business firms that produce products and services but also to government agencies and nonprofit organizations as well. Thus the U.S. Post Office is now competing with many private carriers of mail such as Federal Express for the mail business. And theater groups, social service agencies, colleges, and hospitals have turned to marketing to attract customers and raise more donor money.

I have worked in the marketing field for over 25 years—as teacher, writer, consultant, and trainer—and find continuous challenge in the new problems and issues that arise—whether it is the Chrysler Corporation trying to figure out how to compete more effectively, Apple Computer considering whether to launch a new computer model, or McDonald's deciding whether to introduce a new food product. You will gain the same enthusiasm for marketing as you read Margery Steinberg's excellent discussion on careers in marketing.

Every society must solve the problem of what goods to produce, how to produce them, and how to market them. Careers in marketing will always exist in society, and there is good evidence that they are growing. The ultimate job of marketing people is to produce customer need-satisfaction, otherwise the customers won't come back. So if you like people, if you want to understand their needs, and if you want to create offers that will satisfy their needs, a career in marketing is for you.

Philip Kotler
Northwestern University

PREFACE

How would you like to become part of one of the fastest growing, most in demand, increasingly important areas of the business world? Do you want to prepare for a job that is challenging, creative, and holds the promise of high personal and professional growth? If so read on, for no matter what career you choose, what business you select, or what company you work for, marketing will play a more and more prominent role in your life. Not only has the field grown enormously in the last few years owing to new developments in understanding of the process, but business has placed a greater emphasis on the marketing function in response to our highly competitive environment. The field of marketing offers a dynamic, challenging, creative, and stimulating career. It also has its share of frustration and routine, but the energy level is such that the excitement usually wins out.

We hope to be able to convey some of that excitement to you as you read this book. Leaf through and glance at the career areas that interest you most, then look at some of the others for comparison. The chapter on education is focused primarily on the undergraduate level, but we have included information on advanced degrees as well.

Whether you are in high school and contemplating your future for the first time, employed and considering a career change, or already in the field and seeking advancement, we want you to gain some insight into a profession that is one of that fastest growing today.

You, the reader, will have to accept an active role in the planning and execution of your career, from the moment you first consider the prospect, through college or other preparation, and throughout every position you hold until retirement. A career is an ongoing, dynamic process, one that begins even before your first real job. Because you will spend most of your adult life involved in your career, it is to your benefit to take the time now to learn not only the basic skills needed but also to find out what type of work suits you best and what fields offer the greatest opportunities for self-fulfillment. Not only will you be happier in a career that you like, but people who like their work tend to do better in their jobs and thus are more likely to advance, increasing personal and professional growth, not to mention the financial rewards involved.

Give careful thought to your abilities—are you a people person or a lone ranger? While the business world does require that certain skills be developed, such as the ability to work with others and be a team player, it is important to understand where your strengths lie and how to use them to help you perform to the best of your ability.

It is not the purpose of this book to provide a rigid step-by-step program on how to become a marketer, but rather to present information about the field in a concise, useful manner to help you weigh the pros and cons against your own abilities and aspirations to reach a carefully considered career direction. Use this book as a tool, a source, a springboard for your individual research. Take the information presented here and apply it to yourself, your goals, and your dreams. You, and only you, can decide whether marketing is the right field for you. The best we can do is inform, which we will attempt to do in the most complete and understandable way possible.

It is our hope that we can persuade some of you to join us in this dynamic field and accept the challenge marketing has to offer. Perhaps you will become a major force and make further contributions to the field. We hope so and would like to think this book will play a role in that decision.

To Lew

CONTENTS

CHAPTER 1

WHAT IS MARKETING?

DEBUNKING SOME MYTHS

"Oh, so you're in marketing! Why do you people
_____?" Fill in the blank from the following list:
lie, manipulate, sell shoddy products, make us buy
things we don't want or need, etc. How many times
have you heard words like these or even asked the question yourself? What has the response been? How would
you answer that question? One of the aims of this book
is to help shed some light on popular misconceptions
about marketing—to *market* marketing. A primary
function of marketing is to educate consumers about
products. Persuading people to make informed purchase decisions is how marketing actually works.

To begin with, marketing in and of itself is nothing
more than a powerful tool, and like any tool it can be
misused in the wrong hands. It is a means the marketing professional uses to analyze the market, understand the consumer, and present a product to the

potential benefit of both buyer and seller. In other words, marketing is the bridge between product and customer. By itself, marketing cannot force people to purchase an item they do not need or want (although some less scrupulous persons might wish it could). What consumers often see as the end result may be a reflection of society as it is or as we would like it to be. Don't forget that consumers are the ones who ultimately decide, by voting with their purchase dollars, which products they want on the market.

The American Marketing Association (AMA), the international organization of marketing professionals, offers the following definition of marketing:

> Marketing is the process of planning and executing the conception, pricing, promotion and distribution of ideas, goods, and services to create exchanges that satisfy individual and organizational objectives.

The author likes to expand this definition by noting that marketing is also "responding to the changing environment"—that is, meeting the changing needs of consumers.

In other words, marketing exists within the dynamic context of our social trends and cultural forces, and whatever is happening at the moment, domestic and global. Understanding these activities and their effects —their impact on consumers—is one of the goals of the marketing professional.

A marketer of the author's acquaintance likes to think there is really no magic to marketing, just that the practice of "applied common sense" works its own marvels.

Although marketing is thought of primarily in terms of promotional activity, this is but one of the "four P's" of marketing: Product, Price, Place, and Promotion. These four building blocks, as identified by Philip Kotler, who is one of the foremost authors in the field, describe the basic functions of the marketing process. Not only is marketing more than selling and advertising, so are the careers in the field, such as research director, product manager, project supervisor, assistant buyer, and a whole host of others, which we will discuss later in the book.

As Ralph Waldo Emerson said: ". . .Build a better mousetrap and the world will beat a path to your door. . . ." Product development and management are important pieces of marketing and its ongoing process based on listening to consumers and responding to their needs.

How does the marketer learn what consumers want? Market research is another major area of marketing, and surveys, questionnaires, and correspondence are statistically analyzed to yield consumer preferences and indicate trends. These and other areas of marketing will be discussed in detail in Chapter 3 of this book.

MARKETING IN EVERYDAY LIFE

Most people are more comfortable with the familiar—and marketing is really nothing exotic. See how marketing intertwines with your everyday life from the following examples:

- *Yourself:* From interviewing at a college or for a job, to presentations in class, understanding the consumer—the recipient of your message—will be vital to the success of your endeavor.
- *Your environment:* Political and social causes rely heavily on marketing techniques to ensure their message reaches and involves the greatest number of people who are potential supporters.
- *Your purchases (goods and services):* Every item you use is touched in some way by the four P's: the product itself and its development from concept to concrete, its price and how it was determined, any promotional activity including word of mouth, and finally the place where it is sold and the distribution system that gets it there. Each time you call on a specialist in any field, whether plumber, physician, or pizza parlor, the marketing principle of the right product in the right place at the right time with the right price and the right promotion is employed. Think about it and you'll see how it all works together for you, the consumer.

POSITIONS IN MARKETING

The following are brief descriptions of some of the basic types of jobs that marketers perform.

Marketing Research. Developing and administering questionnaires; collecting, coding, and tabulating data; analyzing the results; and recommending applications and courses of action.

Advertising. Suggesting and developing the approach; creating the artwork; presenting ideas to the client; co-ordinating the production; recommending placement and securing the media space; providing the analysis of cost and reach; coordinating with sales, marketing, and product management.

Public Relations Professional. Monitoring the company name in periodicals and broadcasts; handling consumer inquiries; organizing community or press events; writing and releasing notices to the press.

Salesperson. Presenting the product to consumers (individual or corporate); providing after-sale support with training or other services; disseminating product information; recording sales information for later statistical analysis.

International Marketer. Working within the framework of different legal, social, and cultural traditions; obtaining translations where necessary and consulting native or experienced personnel for guidance in both management of the company as well as marketing expertise.

Retailer. Working for commission on the sales floor; buying merchandise for a department or consumer segment; coordinating and executing displays; analyzing sales figures for merchandising trends and direction; managing the functions of a department, branch, or division.

Consumer Psychologist. Studying the psychological and social aspects of purchasing and consumption; analyzing statistical data and making recommendations for application of the findings.

Product Manager. Coordinating all aspects of an individual item or group of product offerings; overseeing production, advertising, public relations, distribution, sales, and pricing.

Marketing Educator. Teaching groups of business people the latest techniques and practices; contributing to, and staying abreast of, development in the field; working with practitioners to analyze and refine real-world applications.

TYPES OF MARKETING

Within the above disciplines there are further divisions: consumer vs. industrial; products vs. services and ideas; and profit vs. nonprofit/charitable. We will explore each group individually, although in the real world, they can and often do exist in combinations, such as nonprofit consumer services or for-profit industrial ideas.

Although these areas will be treated separately for the sake of clarity, bear in mind that in the real world such distinctions do not always exist. You will likely find, especially in smaller companies, that marketing responsibility encompasses several of the above areas without separating the functions such as advertising and public relations, for example.

One of the trends in marketing is toward reliance on quantification, that is, representing research findings or advertising responses as a numerical value. This tendency results in a scientific approach to marketing, emphasizing mathematical and statistical procedures. Another outcome of this trend is a broader information-based field that appeals to both the qualitative and quantitative mind.

This marketing representative is describing to a customer the various software programs manufactured by her employer. (IBM photo)

CHAPTER 2

CAREER OUTLOOK FOR MARKETERS

Remember how we mentioned in the very beginning of this book that emphasis on marketing has been steadily growing as the business environment has become more competitive? As companies seek to differentiate their products in the marketplace and consumers become better informed, the need for marketing professionals expands. Businesses rely on marketers to guide new product introduction, to observe and analyze the results of an advertising campaign, to read and interpret data on product sales, and most of all to understand consumer needs and how to respond to these needs.

Unless a company can do all these things successfully, it will soon be bypassed for others that are more responsive. More sophisticated and educated than ever, consumers are quick to decide whether a product is or is not worthwhile, and the economic consequences of a product failure are great indeed. New and exciting techniques have been developed to help companies understand the marketplace and satisfy consumer needs. Computers play their role as analytical tools, making it easier than ever to conduct research and interpret large quantities of data. All of this requires an experienced marketer to make it work.

This increasing complexity and speed of marketing decisions reflects changes in the social context. No longer are most items used at home also made at home or purchased locally. Before the days of mass production and communication, a good or service was produced and consumed in small quantities in a small geographical area by a small number of consumers. The purchasers of a good or service were usually personally known by the producer, and their individual requirements could be and frequently were accommodated. These modifications were then incorporated into the entire production run as more requests were received, and word-of-mouth spread the news of these improvements. Actual advertising might have taken the form of a hand-printed sign in a shop window. At this stage, each of the four P's was handled by one person, the producer.

Times have changed drastically, however. The increasing complexity of our society and the distance between producer and consumer demand greater sophistication in our application and coordination of the marketing mix elements of product, price, promotion, and place/distribution.

Marketing has also been one of the fields that offers abundant opportunity for both women and minorities. Whether in sales, research, or product management, the emphasis is on ability, skills, and creativity. In addition, the field of marketing is one of those in which there are several positions rated as having "faster than average" and even "much faster than average" growth potential by the *Occupational Outlook Handbook*, published by the United States Department of Labor (1986-87 edition). The following table is based on information from the *Occupational Outlook Handbook* and indicates the prospects of growth in marketing positions relative to the economy in general.

OUTLOOK FOR SELECTED MARKETING CAREERS THROUGH 1995

Classification	*Outlook*
Advertising	Average
Buyer (Wholesale or Retail)	Average
Display Worker	Average
Education	Faster than average
Graphic Artist	Faster than average
Industrial Designer	Slower than average
Insurance Agent	Slower than average
Manufacturer's Rep	Slower than average
Marketing Researcher	Faster than average
Public Relations Specialist	Much faster than average

Purchasing Agent	Faster than average
Real Estate Agent	Average
Retail Salesperson	Average
Securities Salesperson	Much faster than average
Wholesale Salesperson	Faster than average

Source: Occupational Outlook Handbook, 1986–1987 edition (Washington, D.C., U.S. Government Printing Office, Bureau of Labor Statistics, 1986).

CHAPTER 3

MARKETING FIELDS

Now that you know a little more about marketing in general, it's time to find out what marketers actually do. We will describe typical jobs and their titles, from entry level to top executive. At the end of each field, you will find the names and addresses of the major professional organizations specific to that field, and where appropriate we have included the title of any publications available on careers in the field. Call or write them directly for information on those that interest you. Most will gladly assist someone new to—or just interested in—their specialty.

RESEARCH

Market research is that branch of marketing concerned with finding out why and how. Why was a purchase made? How often? Would it be purchased again? Why not? Where was the purchase made and why? What were the important attributes of the product—

13

was it price, quality, place, or some combination? To what extent was price important? Place? What other factors influenced that purchase? Was it advertising? If so, where were the ads?

How do we obtain the answers to these "why" questions? How do we get consumers to answer these accurately and meaningfully? How do we make sure we're asking the right questions? How do we implement our findings? All of these are the territory of the market researcher.

Jobs and Job Titles

Field Coordinator. Oversees the field personnel who actively collect data, whether administering questionnaires in a shopping center, conducting telephone surveys, or observing focus groups. Ensures that accurate interview and research techniques are being employed, often codes and tabulates data, monitors the project's progress, and reports any abnormalities or unusual situations.

Project Manager. Handles the implementation of the entire research project from methodology to questionnaire design; oversees activity of field coordinators; obtains computer services for statistical analysis; interprets findings and produces reports for presentation to client.

Account Representative/Account Executive. Directs client contact; obtains customers by presenting appropriate research technique for the situation; interprets client needs and represents client to project manager; acts as liaison between client and project team, keeping client informed of progress and preliminary findings; provides support to both client and project team at meetings.

Research Specialist. Generally operates in the context of an advertising agency or in-house marketing/advertising department within a large corporation; is an expert in statistics, research design, and mathematical modeling; oversees all research activity; works with project managers to ensure suitability of methodology and statistical approach as well as validity of findings.

References

Marketing Research Association, 111 East Wacker Drive, Suite 600, Chicago, IL 60601. "Employment and Career Opportunities in Marketing Research."

California State Department of Employment, 800 Capitol Mall, Sacramento, CA 95814. Occupational Guide #291: "Market Research Analyst."

Chronicle Guidance Publications, Inc., Moravia, NY 13118. Occupational Brief #254: "Marketing Research Worker."

ADVERTISING

Does the excitement of working on Madison Avenue have you interested in a career in advertising? Do you want to work behind the scenes on a nationally televised commercial? These are only two of the many facets of advertising, and we will present a brief portrait of this glamorous field. If you are seriously considering an advertising career and would like in-depth reporting, we recommend the book in this series entitled *Opportunities in Advertising Careers.*

Jobs and Job Titles

Account Representative, Account Executive. Directs contact with the client; acts as liaison between art department, production department, and client; maintains communications among these groups; represents client's needs to art and production departments; provides interpretive support to client at presentations; is responsible for seeing that client needs are met accurately and on time, which calls for closely following the in-house progress of the campaign.

Media Buyer, Media Coordinator. Manages the purchase and control of large blocks of media time/space, whether in print or broadcast; recommends and allocates this space among clients according to campaign requirements; negotiates favorable billing terms for large, repeat, and/or guaranteed space purchases, which translates into more cost-effectiveness for clients and agency.

Media Analyst. Applies statistical models to audience, circulation, and cost figures to minimize media cost and maximize media effectiveness, as well as provides support for client campaign implementation.

Art Director. Requires an art background, including experience as a graphic or commercial artist; supervises staff of artists, paste-up, and printing/production technicians; develops and recommends artistic strategy and rendition for client campaign, often presenting several for client approval; oversees progression of campaign from rough sketches through final production.

Production Manager. Coordinates mechanical aspects of campaign for print and broadcast media; oversees quality of renditions and final form whether on paper or film or tape.

Specialty Advertising Manager. Recommends and obtains imprinted merchandise appropriate to client campaign; develops strategy and recommends items to be used; obtains sources and monitors production to ensure timely arrival.

Research Specialist. Usually in a large agency or in-house marketing/advertising department; expert in statistical applications, mathematical modeling, project design, and methodology; works with and often obtains outside services; monitors project to ensure accuracy and validity of findings, which are then reported and presented to the client.

Traffic Manager. An ideal starting point because this position interacts with just about every aspect of advertising. The TM coordinates all the jobs in process and monitors their status to ensure that production remains on schedule and deadlines are met.

"But I don't live in New York—how will I ever get started?" Major cities are loaded with advertising agencies, and many towns have their share of small shops willing to lend a hand with an apprenticeship or internship. If you are already in college and are studying in a related area such as marketing or communications, your placement office can be a good source of information on such openings. You can also look around campus at opportunities with the student newspaper or even the publicity department of the school itself for a chance to gain valuable experience assisting with advertising or related functions.

References

American Association of Advertising Agencies, 200 Park Avenue, New York, NY 10017. Pamphlet: "The Copywriter."

American Advertising Federation, 1400 K Street N.W., Suite 1000, Washington, D.C. 20005.

Business/Professional Advertising Association, 205 East 42nd Street, New York, NY 10017.

Opportunities in Advertising Careers. Vocational Guidance Manuals Career Horizons, Division of National Textbook Co., 4255 W. Touhy Avenue, Lincolnwood, IL 60646.

Advertising Career Directory. Career Publishing Corp., 505 Fifth Avenue, New York, NY 10017. (An excellent overview of the field, with detailed information on each function and chapters written by advertising professionals.)

Catalyst, 14 East 60th Street, New York, NY 10222. Booklet: "Advertising."

Education Council of the Graphic Arts Industry, Inc. 4615 Forbes Avenue, Pittsburgh, PA 15213. Booklet: "Careers in Graphic Communications."

Looking Forward to a Career: Advertising. Bob Larranga. Dillon Press, Inc., 500 South 3rd Street, Minneapolis, MN 55415.

Science Research Associates, 259 East Erie Street, Chicago, IL 60611. Pamphlet #371: "Advertising Account Executives."

The Fashion Institute of Design and Merchandising, 323 West Eighth Street, Los Angeles, CA 90014. Pamphlet: "Fashion Industry Careers."

American Advertising Federation, 1225 Connecticut Avenue N.W., Washington, DC 20036. Various career pamphlets.

American Association of Advertising Agencies, 200 Park Avenue, New York, NY 10017. Pamphlets: "The Significance of Advertising," "Advertising: A Guide to Careers in Advertising," and "Selected Bibliography of Books on Advertising."

Chronicle Guidance Publications, Inc., Moravia, NY 13118. Occupational Brief #113: "Advertising Agency Occupations."

Your Career in Advertising. George Johnson. Julian Messner, Division of Simon & Schuster, Inc., 1230 Avenue of the Americas, New York, NY 10020.

Educational Council of the Graphic Arts Industry, Inc., 4615 Forbes Avenue, Pittsburgh, PA 15213. Booklet: "Careers in Graphic Communications."

PUBLIC RELATIONS

You've probably heard the term *public relations*, but do you know what it really means and how and why companies use it? Public relations (PR) is, literally, the relationship of the company with the public it serves including consumers, employees, stockholders, and the community. As companies are in the public eye, they make every effort to ensure that the public is aware of the positive aspects of their business, which might otherwise go unnoticed. This is the task of the PR department—to see that the press is notified of new product introductions, favorable investment performance, employees promoted or hired, company-supported community projects, and similar newsworthy events.

Jobs and Job Titles

PR Assistant. An entry level position at which one performs mostly behind-the-scenes activities such as writing routine press releases; coordinating luncheons and special events by reserving the room or site, ordering the meal, arranging for the speaker, ensuring attendance, and providing press coverage; and basically attending to the details involved in carrying out the corporate or client's public relations goals.

PR Manager. Develops and implements the PR program at the corporate level (or for clients), coordinating the activities of PR assistants with those of other departments.

Community Relations Manager. Usually in the largest corporations, this position is directly involved with activities in the community in which the corporation is located. By lending financial and/or personnel support to community-based causes, the corporation helps those organizations remain viable and contributes to the stability of the community. In addition, the corporation gains credibility and favorable press coverage for its civic-mindedness.

Community Relations Director. Evaluates various opportunities for community involvement; works with representatives from those organizations to develop appropriate programs for corporate sponsorship.

References

Public Relations Society of America, Inc., 845 Third Avenue, New York, NY 10022.

Public Relations Career Directory. Career Publishing Corp., 505 Fifth Avenue, Suite 1003, New York, NY 10017.

SALES AND SALES MANAGEMENT

This is the area most people think of when you mention "marketing." In a sales job you are representing your company and its products to your customer on a one-to-one basis. You must not only know your products and how they perform; you must know those of your competitors as well and how they compare to yours.

Jobs and Job Titles

Market Representative, Account Executive, Salesperson, Sales Representative. Entry level often involves a training program in the larger corporations. In smaller companies, an apprenticeship of sorts is more the rule, accompanying an experienced salesperson at first, then moving on to one's own territory to visit clients and develop new business.

Sales Manager (Area, Product or Product Line, Group, District, Regional, National). Directing the activities of the sales force involves coordinating with other departments such as marketing and advertising so that special promotions and new products are supported in the field. Monitoring sales performance and forecasting sales figures are also part of the job.

Sales Director (Area, Group, Product or Product Line, District, Regional, National). Oversees the sales activities of several groups or sales managers and is often responsible for their profitability. Ensures the cooperation of other departments with the sales effort, as well as sale's support of promotional activities. Vice-president of sales or sales and marketing (area, group, product line, district, region, or national) is often the next step up the ladder after serving as sales director.

References

American Society of Professional Salesmen, 1000 Vermont Avenue N.W., Washington, DC 20005. Booklets: "The Professional Salesman" and "Opportunities in Selling."

Sales and Marketing Executives International, 330 West 42nd Street, New York, NY 10036. Booklet: "The Salesman—Ambassador of Progress."

National Retail Merchants Association, 100 West 31st Street, New York, NY 10001. Booklet: "Your Opportunities in Retailing."

American Marketing Association, 250 South Wacker Drive, Chicago, IL 60606. Booklet: "Careers in Marketing."

The Union Central Life Insurance Company, Box 179, Cincinnati, OH 45201. Booklet: "How to Select a Sales Career."

INTERNATIONAL MARKETING

International marketing is coming of age as our business environment is more worldwide than ever. With today's emphasis on multinational corporations and balance of trade between countries, the international marketer is right in the thick of things as they occur in the global marketplace.

International marketers generally begin their careers in another area of the marketing function and transfer to the international department after gaining experience in one or more aspects of marketing. One way to speed up the process is to establish fluency in a foreign language, specifically that of a country in which your company does business.

Jobs and Job Titles

International Specialist. Usually an experienced marketer with knowledge of the country in which the company is interested. This person should be familiar not only with the language but the culture and legal climate as well. Often, people in this position are native to the foreign country and have lived and worked in America to gain experience in this market. This does not preclude an American person working in international marketing, but it serves to point up the importance of immersion in the other country's culture.

Director of International Marketing. Coordinates all overseas marketing activities, generally living and working abroad. This position frequently takes on diplomatic overtones as business relationships in and with other countries are frequently as carefully negotiated as political ties.

References

Numerous international groups and organizations can supply you with more information on business and marketing opportunities abroad.

Areas closely related to marketing include advertising, public relations, sales, and retailing and merchandising. (Pattis Group photo)

RETAILING AND MERCHANDISING

Retailing and merchandising are more than just selling; planning and forecasting are a big part of the job.

A career in retailing used to consist of a few positions, beginning in the stockroom and progressing to salesperson on the floor, then moving up to store manager. The only promotion after that required buying the store. Times have indeed changed, and today one can work for a regional or national chain or one that specializes in a particular type of merchandise. You can specialize, too, in operations or merchandising, and many store executives have experience in a broad spectrum of store functions.

Jobs and Job Titles

Buyer (Assistant, Junior, Senior). Beginning as a junior buyer, one serves as an apprentice and learns the groundwork of the retailing business, such as calculating open-to-buy and dealing with different manufacturers, under the direction of the buyer (senior or assistant, depending on the size of the company).

As assistant buyer, one is given more responsibility while still under the direction of another more experienced buyer. Often the assistant will work with a particular manufacturer or merchandise line.

Once the position of buyer or senior buyer is attained, one is usually responsible for purchases for a single department or merchandise segment and oversees the activities of any junior or assistant buyers in that department.

Department Manager. Coordinates buying activities for the given department; oversees day-to-day staffing, customer service, efficiency, orderliness, and merchandise display; responsible for longer-term buying projections and performance statistics, including the profitability of the department.

Merchandise Manager. This position oversees the purchasing of items in a broad group, such as housewares or men's apparel, and coordinates activities between departments under that category. Also responsible for purchase and performance analysis, as well as the profitability of the merchandise group.

Store/Branch Manager. Handles operations for all departments and merchandise lines at a given location. Coordinates purchase and performance activities between buyers and managers and is responsible for profitability of the branch.

Regional (Function) Manager. Oversees operations of several stores or branches for a given function such as purchasing or display. Responsible for analyzing and accommodating local preferences and conditions and profitability of the region.

General Manager. Based at headquarters and responsible for all operations and profitability of the regions or branches.

Vice-President (Function or Region). Also based at headquarters, oversees all function-related or regional activities. Again, profitability is a responsibility. Usually found in the larger retail organizations.

References

Association of Buying Offices, 100 West 31st Street, New York, NY 10001.

National Retail Merchants Association, 100 West 31st Street, New York, NY 10001. Booklet: "Your Opportunities in Retailing."

Superintendent of Documents, U.S. Government Printing Office, Washington, DC 20402. Bulletin #1875-53: "Retail Trade Sales Workers."

Science Research Associates, 259 East Erie Street, Chicago, IL 60611. Pamphlet #239: "Retail Salespeople."

California State Department of Employment, Sacramento, CA. Occupational Guide #242: "Retail Store Manager."

The Fashion Institute of Design and Merchandising, 790 Market Street, San Francisco, CA 94102. Pamphlet: "Fashion Industry Careers" and booklet: "Career Opportunities: The Fashion Institute of Design and Merchandising."

U.S. Department of Labor, Bureau of Labor Statistics, Occupational Outlook Service, GAO Building, Washington, DC 20212. Bulletin #1875-28: "Buyers."

Science Research Associates, Chicago, IL 60611. Pamphlet #284: "Buyers."

Looking Forward to a Career in Fashion. Margot Siegel. Dillon Press, Inc., 500 South Third Street, Minneapolis, MN 55415.

Your Career in the Fashion Industry. VGM Career Books, a division of National Textbook Company, 4255 West Touhy Avenue, Lincolnwood, IL 60646.

CONSUMER PSYCHOLOGY

Consumer psychology attempts to understand how consumers make purchase decisions—what they buy and why. This area often works closely with market research to develop questionnaires that will elicit accurate responses and develop meaningful data.

Jobs and Job Titles

Analyst. Usually in an advertising agency or a large consumer package-goods company, this position provides understanding of what motivates consumers to purchase an item. This information helps the company decide how best to reach its intended customer, as well as give insight to what people want in a product.

Specialist. This field is prime for entrepreneurs, and those who are involved are often research-oriented. A popular career choice in this area is education.

Educator. Many consumer behaviorists can be found teaching marketing and consumer behavior at the college level while pursuing their research in the field. This can be an ideal position for the consumer psychologist.

PRODUCT MANAGEMENT

This area of marketing requires a broad understanding of other business functions such as production, accounting, and distribution. You will work closely with people from these and other departments to manage your new product's development, the test marketing, refining, formal introduction, and roll-out. These same groups will also be necessary to keep your existing product on the market, updating it as necessary to meet changing demand and ultimately retiring it when the market for it declines. At the same time, the new product manager is introducing a replacement for the retired product.

Jobs and Job Titles

Assistant Product Manager. Entry level position working with the product manager, handling only certain product-related functions that are often in the form of special projects such as a cooperative advertising sales promotion.

Product Manager. This position has responsibility for all product-related functions and must see to it that activities are coordinated and that the product involved stays aligned with corporate goals. Profit accountability begins here.

Group Manager. Oversees a line of related products and their managers, with responsibility similar to that of the product manager on a larger scale.

Regional Manager. Responsible for all product-related or line-related activities in a given geographical area. Must also ensure that the activities of the product and/or group managers adhere to strategic goals for the area.

Division Manager. Handles the complete line of related products or product groups on a national level. Accountable for productivity as well as profitability on a national level, this position coordinates the activities of several group and/or regional managers.

Division Vice-President. Ultimate product responsibility rests here along with corporate goal setting and strategy implementation.

SERVICES MARKETING

When a product is not a tangible product, how do you demonstrate that yours is better? More than ever, our economy is based on services like advertising, consulting, or word processing rather than on hard goods or products. As technology improves and manufacturing decreases, there is less demand for products and more demand for the after-sales support and follow-through that helps to differentiate one company from another. Although similar to product marketing in function and areas of responsibility, the challenge of services marketing lies in the intangible nature of a service and the ongoing usage of this kind of "product."

Jobs and Job Titles

Manager (Assistant). Much like its counterpart in product marketing, this position must coordinate all activities (promotional, production, etc.) for the given service. In addition, the services marketing manager must also ensure that follow-up and after-sale support is thorough and effective in order to maintain a positive relationship with the customers.

Group Manager. Oversees several related services and coordinates all related activities. Sees to it that the efforts of the services managers are cohesive and are pulling in the same direction. Responsible for productivity and profitability of the total group.

Division Manager. Handles the coordination of several groups of related services, again ensuring that corporate goals are met and that activities are unified.

Regional Manager. Similar to the division manager, but for an assigned geographical area. Must also ensure responsiveness to regional differences while complying with the corporate strategy.

Vice-President. Encompasses responsibility for several divisions or regions. Oversees primarily the financial and productivity areas, relying on the lower levels to provide follow-up and responsiveness to the consumer.

NONPROFIT MARKETING

There are many national nonprofit associations, and these organizations tend to be smaller and more localized than their counterparts in industry. Of necessity, staff size is often minimal, and each position frequently holds more responsibility than might otherwise be expected. There is usually a high degree of interaction with the community—from individuals to industries. As a result, a job with a nonprofit organization or agency can be exceptionally challenging as well as fulfilling.

Jobs and Job Titles

Assistant or Coordinator. The entry level position working with the marketing or development director. Responsible for the nuts and bolts of a particular campaign, whether for membership or fundraising. Often involved in special projects requiring research and interpretive skills.

Marketing Director. Must develop the campaign and oversee its implementation, often coordinating the activities of a large staff of volunteers. Frequently requires specialized knowledge of nonprofit associations and community relations. Handles public relations if the organization does have a PR department or consultant.

Development Director. Fund-raising responsibility rests here, requiring skill in market development and experience in financial goal setting. Must cultivate close ties with the community, both corporate and individual. Also works with a volunteer staff and coordinates activities.

Executive Director. The ultimate nonprofit position with responsibility for all functions of the organization from fund raising to public relations to community involvement. Requires not only good business sense but also an outgoing, gregarious personality.

Reference

National Society for Fund-Raising Executives, Washington, D.C.

DIRECT MARKETING

Direct marketing involves reaching the consumers without using a retailer. This type of marketing takes many forms, some you are probably already familiar with. No doubt you've received catalogs through the mail and possibly even had telemarketing calls from computers. These are but two of the many ways producers of products and services can use to reach the consumer directly. One of the newest methods ties in the popularity of cable television. Called "electronic shopping," this medium allows the consumer to make credit-card purchases via cable (usually telephone lines) through services that offer a wide variety of products and ship directly to the consumer.

Jobs and Job Titles

Specialist. In this position you would be responsible for promoting the use of your company's shopping service to both the consumer and the producer. Determining which promotional methods would be most effective and implementing a campaign to reach your market goal are important objectives of the specialist.

Manager. Similar to the position of product manager: sets goals for market share and profitability. Also handles the administrative functions of coordinating with other important areas like advertising, sales, and research and development.

Director. Typically a semitechnical position requiring thorough knowledge of the latest innovations in electronics and software as well as awareness of consumer response to these developments. The ability to apply these updates or recommend modifications to increase the appeal of current offerings would enhance performance in this position.

References

Direct Selling Association, 1730 M Street N.W., Suite 610, Washington, DC 20006.

Direct Marketing Association, 6 E. 43rd St., New York, NY 10017.

INDUSTRIAL (BUSINESS-TO-BUSINESS) MARKETING

What's different when the consumer is a corporation? One difference is that you are often selling to a group, and you must understand the dynamics of that group. Or, in other cases, you must penetrate several layers of people before reaching the decision maker. While there are similarities to consumer marketing, businesspeople need to be treated differently, as is appropriate when single purchases represent large amounts of money and major budget items. Business-to-business marketing also tends to be more technical in nature and requires technical product knowledge often exceeding that of consumer marketers. In many cases your customer will know as much about your product as you do. As your product can affect how people perform their jobs, each purchase is carefully considered.

Jobs and Job Titles

Account Representative/Sales Representative. As in consumer marketing, this position involves calling on existing and potential customers for the purpose of persuading them to purchase your company's product. However, in industrial marketing you will most likely be talking to a group of people who are all involved in the purchase decision and will have individual criteria for the product or service you represent. In many cases, you will need a technical background in order to fully understand your customers' needs.

Marketing Manager. Responsible for the overall marketing effort for a company's product offerings. Also responsible for the productivity and profitability of the marketing activities. Must also be familiar with the industry in general and the needs of its customers.

Sales Manager. Oversees the activities of the sales force and coordinates those activities with the other related departments such as advertising and marketing. Has profit and productivity responsibility for the sales effort. Often accompanies the salesperson on calls to major clients and establishes business relationships with these customers.

Divisional Sales/Marketing Manager. Coordinates the sales/marketing activities within a given product-line group or geographic region. Responsible for profitability and productivity, setting market and/or sales goals, and monitoring progress of the company and its competitors in the field.

References

See the listing under Sales and Sales Management. Also check headings for individual industries in the *Encyclopedia of Associations.*

MARKETING EDUCATION

Teaching at the college level is available in all areas (professional and geographic) and offers an exciting opportunity to share and apply learned marketing skills. Teaching requires advanced degrees, an MBA or equivalent in a related field, plus enrollment in a Ph.D. program.

Jobs and Job Titles

Adjunct Lecturer. Usually a part-time position, often evenings, this position generally requires only an MBA or master's degree at most schools.

Instructor. The entry level designation for full-time faculty, this position requires enrollment in a Ph.D. program as demonstration of serious commitment to the field.

Assistant Professor. Promotion to this level is usually contingent upon completion of the Ph.D. coursework but is frequently granted when the doctorate is earned.

Associate Professor. Must have Ph.D. (or equivalent) and contingent upon contribution to the school and the field.

Full Professor. Requires continued service, high-level research, and involvement in the profession.

Department Chair. An administrative position, this is often rotated among department members.

Dean. Administrator of the school or department of business, often in conjunction with teaching. Further advancement takes place either in administration or in professional activities, such as publishing.

References

Occupational Outlook Handbook in Brief, Regional Office.

U.S. Department of Labor, BLS, Occupational Outlook Service, GAO, Washington, DC 20212. Bulletin #1875-48: "College and University Teachers."

CONSULTING

Consulting is available in almost any area of marketing and is limited only by your skills and experience. This is not an entry level position, but after developing your expertise, consulting offers an excellent opportunity to see many companies in action and learn how a variety of industries operate.

Jobs and Job Titles

Consultant. Whether independent or in partnership, flexibility and independence are major advantages, along with the opportunity to be your own boss. Consulting can be and often is a second job until enough of a practice is built up to support full-time activity.

References

See the previous headings for the particular sector of the marketing industry that is of interest to you.

This marketing executive uses a regional information network to perfom such tasks as business planning, scheduling meetings, and electronically distributing documents. (IBM photo)

CHAPTER 4

THE REWARDS OF MARKETING

One of the best ways to find out what people like about their jobs is to ask them. Talk to everyone you know who is in the field and even a few people you don't know. An effective way to approach people in a position you'd like to know more about is simply to call or write, indicating your interest in pursuing a job in their field and asking for a few minutes of their time to ask their advice (at their convenience, of course). Set up an appointment to discuss their job, how they got started, features of the job, and what course you might follow to attain a similar position yourself. Read some of the articles in recent publications to learn current practices and recent developments, issues, and trends related to the field. *Sales and Marketing Management*, *Marketing Media Decisions*, the *Marketing News*, as well as the marketing or business sections in *Time* and *Newsweek* will all lend background to your investigation. *Business Week's Careers* is also a good source of information for the undergraduate or recent graduate.

FINANCIAL REWARDS

Surely the most common question about a job is "What kind of money can I make?" Naturally there are great variations from one region to another, even between companies, making it even more difficult to present an accurate picture of potential earnings. However, we spoke to marketing people in many different positions and in different parts of the country to verify published figures, and we came up with the following ranges for marketers with experience. Of course, entry level salaries will be much lower (as they are in any field) but chances for advancement in marketing are good. You should be able to increase your earnings and gain experience during your first few years, which will make you promotable and marketable. Here are the findings of our salary research—remember they are approximate, but they should give you an idea of the ranges you can expect.

AREA OF MARKETING	SALARY RANGE
Research	$20,000– 40,000
Advertising	15,000– 55,000
Public Relations	21,000– 42,500
Sales and Sales Management	17,000–150,000
International	25,000– 60,000
Retailing	18,000– 50,000
Consumer Behavior	22,000– 65,000
Product Management	22,000– 55,000

AREA OF MARKETING	SALARY RANGE
Industrial	18,000–100,000
Services	22,000– 60,000
Nonprofit	23,000– 65,000
Consulting	25,000–150,000
Education	22,000– 48,000

INTRINSIC AND EMOTIONAL REWARDS

The intangible rewards that come from solving problems and serving consumers often override the financial aspects. If you feel good about your work and can recognize the positive impact you can have on the products and services offered to the consuming public, you will have something money alone cannot buy. All too often we get caught up in the idea that a bigger salary, house, or car are the only rewards of a career. Personal growth, professional development, and positive feelings about one's career are frequently missing, even from those who would seem to have it all. Marketing is a field that lends itself to intrinsic rewards, as well as financial ones. It is what *you* make it, so make the most of it.

Getting the right amount of education and training is important for a successful career in marketing. (American Marketing Association photos)

CHAPTER 5

EDUCATION AND TRAINING

How much education is enough? What should you study? What other disciplines are important? There are also differences in opinion between those who emphasize education and others who prefer experience in the field (the school of hard knocks). Still others feel that only a business education is appropriate for a career in marketing, while some believe a liberal arts background is better-rounded. Who has the answers to these questions? Nobody and everybody. However, only you can decide what's better for you and your career. Let's look at some of the possibilities.

BACHELOR'S DEGREE

The aim of an undergraduate education is to develop an individual who can think independently, communicate effectively, and who has been exposed to a common body of knowledge that forms the basis of our culture as well as that of others. At this level the emphasis is on the broad concepts, the understanding of how and why a particular theory functions, and the foundations of various disciplines rather than the depth of the specialist. Another outcome is a systematic approach to problem solving—a rational, logical process rather than unfocused, random methods—and the ability to apply basic mathematical and communication skills.

Even though you may be absolutely fascinated by marketing and want to spend your college career immersed in the field, restrain yourself and get a well-rounded education. This is your chance to become an educated individual. The importance of the liberal arts cannot be understated; develop your communications abilities, work on the analytical skills, and learn as much as you can about our world. In fact, most good undergraduate business programs require a balanced course of study, and actual coursework in marketing generally does not begin until the junior year, after you have already been exposed to other disciplines. Remember, nothing exists in a vacuum. Even though a particular course, such as art history, may not seem relevant to you as a business major, it is still a part of the cultural context in which you will operate as a marketer and will inevitably take its place in your professional development.

Business people cite communications and interpersonal skills as the areas college graduates most need to improve. Writing is an extremely important skill, and the time to learn is while you have experts to teach you—in school. If you have trouble with grammar, spelling, or sentence structure, now is the time to get help. Enroll in a remedial class if your school offers one. Remember, a poorly written document detracts from your professional image as much as does wearing scruffy clothes to the office.

School is also the place to learn by making mistakes —take advantage of campus organizations to develop your leadership style and refine your people skills. Learn how to work with other individuals and groups; develop some diplomacy and practice using tact—you will find it much more effective and much less offensive than unbridled bluntness. Remember: "It's not what you say but how you say it." You can accomplish more with other people when they are not put off by your manner.

The college and local chapters of the American Marketing Association are good places to begin and may be augmented by membership in specialized societies in management, public relations, advertising, and the like. Belonging to such groups as an undergraduate also reflects favorably on your commitment to the field and is not overlooked by potential employers.

THE AACSB PROGRAM

The American Assembly of Collegiate Schools of Business (AACSB), a nonprofit association of educational institutions, businesses, and other groups, is "devoted to the promotion and improvement of higher education in business administration and management." The AACSB is recognized by the U.S. Department of Education as the sole national accrediting agency of bachelor's and master's degree programs in business administration.

This organization promotes the usage of standardized and accurate descriptions of courses and programs in business, and member schools must meet strict criteria in faculty standards, program quality, and available resources. Many nonmember schools also pattern their course offerings after the AACSB model in order to offer a course of study with exposure to all facets of the business world while allowing for a professional concentration such as marketing.

Here is the recommended course of study for marketing majors, as set forth by the AACSB:

Total Credits Required: 120

Freshman Year—Required Credits: 30
    English Composition (6)
    Principles of Accounting (6)
    Pre-Calculus Math (3)
    Calculus (3)
    Introduction to Computing/Programming (3)
    Liberal Arts Electives (9)

Sophomore Year—Required Credits: 32
    Principles of Economics (6)
    Legal Environment of Business (3)
    Quantitative Analysis for Business Decisions (3)
    Business Statistics (4)
    Liberal Arts Electives (16)

Junior Year—Required Credits: 30
  Processes and Functions of Management (3)
  Organizational Behavior (3)
  Principles of Marketing (3)
  Principles of Finance (3)
  Courses in Professional Concentration/Marketing (6)
  Examples include:
   • Consumer Behavior
   • Introduction to Advertising
   • Personal Selling
   • International Marketing
  Marketing Electives (12), chosen from any marketing courses not taken as requirements, and availability at your school may vary.

Senior Year—Required Credits: 30
  Business Policy (3)
  Courses in Professional Concentration/Marketing (15)
  Examples include:
   • Sales/Marketing Management
   • Marketing Strategy
   • Industrial Marketing
   • Retailing/Merchandise Management
   • New Product Management
   • High-Tech Marketing
   • Advertising Strategy
   • Public Relations
  Electives (12), again selected from any marketing courses not taken in fulfillment of requirements. Examples include:
   • Services Marketing
   • Health Care Marketing
   • Direct Marketing

THE MBA

With good reason, one of the most often asked questions is "Do I really need an MBA?" It follows that the next question is "Do most companies require one?"

In most situations, the answer to such questions is "It depends"—on your undergraduate education, your employer's requirements, but mostly on your personal and professional goals. What kind of work do you want to do and for what size company? Do you have a bachelor's degree in business? If so, did you concentrate in marketing? If you are employed in the field, you can determine better how much an MBA would enhance your knowledge and ability to perform your current job or perhaps even prepare you for advancement.

The MBA is a longer, harder look at the quantitative skills; the statistical techniques are more sophisticated, the analytical approaches are more complex. This is the level at which you concentrate on the field. Whether you generalize or specialize in marketing may depend on the nature of your undergraduate degree. Someone who concentrated in marketing at the undergraduate level may wish to round out that education by taking a generalist business degree or an MBA in finance or management information systems (MIS).

This is a good time to point out that most good MBA programs require business experience, preferably at least two years' worth, prior to entering the program.

This gives you the opportunity to gain some exposure to concrete examples of concepts you will encounter during your graduate studies, as well as allow you to test the waters to make certain the MBA is right for you.

Although the MBA has become increasingly popular due to its perceived glamour and the higher salaries some graduates command, a word of caution is in order. Because the sheer number of MBAs awarded has grown so rapidly, the value of the degree to any person or company is more and more related to individual circumstances than to the degree itself. Above the entry level, an MBA is certainly desirable and may be required for advancement to upper management in certain companies. At the very least it should help you refine the decision-making skills you have developed at the undergraduate level and on the job—if not provide you with a whole set of new skills.

In addition, if the company requires you to have an MBA, or at least desires it, there may be some financial assistance, such as tuition abatement, to you as an employee. This is another reason to consider working for several years before pursuing the degree.

Does an MBA lead to a higher salary? Generally, but not always. What is more likely to occur is that enhanced job performance is rewarded and promotions earned more quickly than without the MBA. Also, more doors may be opened and more opportunities available with the degree than without. Again, your individual goals come into play by suggesting which direction you should take, and only you can decide whether to pursue this form of graduate education. For serious marketing practitioners, however, the MBA is a valuable tool and should be viewed as such.

Within the schools granting the MBA there is considerable variation in teaching methods—each with advantages and drawbacks—the effectiveness of which will vary with the student. These techniques run the gamut from full lecture to full case method, with every possible combination along the way. A full investigation of the teaching philosophy of any MBA programs you might consider is necessary to ensure optimal gain from the educational experience. Some schools offer learn-by-doing (also called Co-op) opportunities with local businesses or internships in conjunction with established training programs, both of which provide unique hands-on experience in applying the skills and concepts learned in the academic side of the program. Ask about such possibilities when considering an MBA program. Again, the appropriateness will depend on individual circumstances, personal objectives, and work experience.

The following is a listing of the typical courses you may expect to encounter in an MBA program. The number of credits appears in parentheses next to course listings.

Basic Courses:
  Management: Theory and Practice (3)
  Introduction to Management Information Systems (3)

Financial Accounting (3)
Quantitative Decision Methods (3)
Managerial Statistics (3)
Marketing Management (3)
Economic Analysis for Managers (3)

Intermediate Courses:
Human Factors in Management (3)
Managerial Accounting (3)
Corporate Finance (3)

Advanced Courses:
Organizational Strategy and Policy
Business and Society

Some schools offer what is known as the "executive" or "intensive" MBA program. Sometimes given on company premises, this type of program is geared toward the student who is already heavily involved in the business world and may have achieved mid- to upper-management status without the benefit of specialized education. Such a program usually schedules classes on weekends or during brief but intense periods dedicated only to academic activity. Some require sponsorship by one's company and may be tailored to the needs of that particular corporation; others are open to all.

As far as companies requiring an MBA is concerned, a general rule is: the larger the corporation, the more likely it is to prefer that its management-level employees possess an advanced degree. There are always exceptions, of course, and many large corporations make it easier for their employees to obtain the degree by offering such benefits as tuition reimbursement and flex-time to accommodate class hours. Suffice it to say that you may find it easier to obtain a challenging career position if you have the MBA behind you.

Another thorny issue is the prominence of the school granting your MBA. Again, only you can weigh the potential benefits against your academic and financial abilities as well as your personal and professional goals. Do you want to be the next whiz-kid vice-president at a top New York advertising agency? Or is it your ambition to be the head of market research at a major consumer goods manufacturer?

THE DOCTORATE

Did you ever wonder why someone would pursue an education at this level? Or has the idea intrigued you but you didn't know how you might use the degree? You can teach your subject at the college level and be stimulated by other intelligent minds; you can consult with companies, employing your expertise in the field; you can conduct research in your area and contribute to the body of knowledge; or you can do just about any combination thereof. One of the attractions of obtaining the Ph.D. is the flexibility it affords in a career choice, as well as the intellectual challenge and the stimulation of being on the cutting edge of new developments in your chosen field.

The Ph.D. program is usually specifically tailored to

the individual's interests, as well as those of the faculty in the department. If you are interested in a Ph.D. degree, there is a list in the appendix of those schools offering such a program. Contact the department head directly for the information you need.

This marketing student gives a presentation on consumer response to a survey she conducted. (DePaul University photo)

CHAPTER 6

A CAREER IN MARKETING: HONEST WORK

Before we go any further, let's discuss an extremely important issue—that of ethics, a code of conduct. Remember in the beginning of the book where we attempted to address some of the negative stereotypes of marketers? Well, the American Marketing Association (AMA), an organization dedicated to professionalism in marketing, has adopted a code of ethics to guide all those in the field in its practice and conduct. The code as it appears here was approved and adopted by the AMA on June 12, 1987. As you read this document, consider how it opposes those negative stereotypes we talked about and in their place promotes a positive, honest approach to business in general. This code of ethics is quoted in its entirety.

RESPONSIBILITIES OF THE MARKETER

Marketers must accept responsibility for the consequences of their activities and make every effort to ensure that their decisions, recommendations, and actions function to identify, serve, and satisfy all relevant publics—customers, organizations, and society.

The marketer's professional conduct must be guided by:

1. The basic rule of professional ethics: not knowingly to do harm;
2. The adherence to all applicable laws and regulations;
3. The accurate representation of their education, training, and experience; and
4. The active support, practice, and promotion of this Code of Ethics.

HONESTY AND FAIRNESS

Marketers shall uphold and advance the integrity, honor, and dignity of the marketing profession by:

1. Being honest with consumers, clients, employees, suppliers, distributors, and the public;
2. Communicating in a truthful and forthright manner;
3. Not knowingly participating in any conflict of interest; and

4. Establishing equitable fee schedules, including the payment or receipt of compensation only for usual, customary, and legal marketing exchanges.

RIGHTS AND DUTIES OF PARTIES IN THE MARKETING EXCHANGE PROCESS

Participants in the marketing exchange process should be able to expect that:

1. Products and services offered are safe and fit for their intended uses;
2. Communications about offered products and services are not deceptive;
3. All parties intend to discharge their obligations, financial and otherwise in good faith; and
4. Appropriate internal forums and mechanisms exist for equitable adjustment, and/or redress of grievances concerning purchases.

It is understood that the above would include *but is not limited to*, the following:

In the area of product development and management,

- disclosure of all substantial risks associated with product or service use,
- identification of any product component substitution that might materially change the product or impact on the buyer's purchase decision,
- identification and approval of extra-cost added features.

In the area of promotions,

- avoidance of false and misleading advertising,
- rejection of high-pressure selling tactics, such as the use of associates to mislead, or of bait and switch to manipulate,
- repudiation of overstating inventory needs or selling the customer product features which are not needed.

In the area of distribution,

- not manipulating the availability of a product for the purpose of exploitation,
- not using coercion in the marketing channel,
- not exerting undue influence over the reseller's choice to handle a product.

In the area of pricing,

- not engaging in price fixing,
- not practicing predatory pricing,
- disclosing the full price associated with any purchase.

In the area of marketing research,

- prohibiting selling or fundraising under the guise of conducting research,
- maintaining research integrity by avoiding misrepresentation and pertinent omission of research data,
- treating outside clients and suppliers fairly.

ORGANIZATIONAL RELATIONSHIPS

Marketers should be aware of how their behavior may influence or impact on the behavior of others in organizational relationships. They should not demand, encourage, or apply coercion to obtain unethical behavior in their relationships with others, such as employees, suppliers, or customers. Marketers should:

1. Apply confidentiality and anonymity in professional relationships with regard to privileged information;
2. Meet their obligations and responsibilities in contracts and mutual agreements in a timely manner;
3. Avoid taking the work of others, in whole or in part, and representing this work as their own or directly benefiting from it without compensation or consent of the originator or owner;
4. Avoid manipulating to take advantage of situations to maximize personal welfare in a way that unfairly deprives or damages the organization or others.

(Reprinted with the permission of the American Marketing Association.)

The code of ethics concludes: "Any AMA member found to be in violation of any provision of this Code of Ethics may have his or her Association membership suspended or revoked."

This code is a far cry from the "buyer beware" approach businesspeople are often accused of practicing. Think about how you might employ this code as both a marketer and a consumer. See how other businesspeople are operating within the guidelines set down in the code and how a company's reputation for honesty and accuracy can also improve its profitability. After all, what kind of product would *you* prefer? What kind of company do you go back to time after time? Won't your customers want the same of you and your company?

Unscrupulous businesspeople may receive media attention (as well as serious punishment) for their misdeeds, but fortunately their activities are usually short-lived. These people are the ones who give business a bad name and whose memory lingers with the consuming public. The overwhelming majority of marketers, however, conduct themselves and their businesses in accordance with the tenets of the code of ethics to the mutual benefit of producer and consumer.

CHAPTER 7

PROFESSIONAL ORGANIZATIONS

The following is a list of associations with professional members in various facets of marketing and related areas. For further information, you may contact the organization directly either by phone or by mail. Most groups welcome inquiries, and some even accept student members. You will notice some industry-specific associations. We have included only a representative group, but you may research any industry of particular interest by consulting the *Encyclopedia of Associations*, which also gives a thumbnail sketch of the aims of the organizations.

Of special interest to marketers in general is the American Marketing Association (AMA), *the* organization for marketing professionals. The AMA has collegiate, local, and national chapters dedicated to furthering the practice of marketing and to educating the public in the ethical conduct of business.

The *Encyclopedia of Associations*, published by Gale Research Company and available in the reference section of most libraries, is a valuable source of information on professional and trade associations. Each entry lists the address of the organization and the name of the current director. It also provides some background information on the group and its focus. Some general categories to check in this publication are: Advertising, Public Relations, Communications, Marketing, Sales, Retailing, Product Management, or any industry of special interest to you.

Academy of Marketing Science
  School of Business Administration
  University of Miami
  P.O. Box 248505
  Coral Gables, Florida 33124

Advertising Club of New York
  155 East 55th Street, Suite 202
  New York, New York 10022
  (212) 935-8080

Advertising Council
  825 Third Avenue
  New York, New York 10022
  (212) 758-0400

Advertising and Marketing International Network
  1 Bank Street
  Stamford, Connecticut 06901
  (203) 327-0890

Advertising Research Foundation
  3 East 54th Street
  New York, New York 10022
  (212) 751-5656

Advertising Women of New York
  153 East 57th Street
  New York, New York 10022
  (212) 593-1950

Affiliated Advertising Agencies International
  2280 South Xanadu Way, Suite 300
  Aurora, Colorado 80014
  (303) 671-8551

American Advertising Federation
  1400 K Street N.W., Suite 1000
  Washington, D.C. 20005
  (202) 898-0089

American Association of Advertising Agencies
  666 Third Avenue, 13th Floor
  New York, New York 10017
  (212) 682-2500

American Marketing Association
  250 South Wacker Drive, Suite 200
  Chicago, Illinois 60606
  (312) 648-0536

American Retail Federation
  1616 H Street, N.W.
  Washington, D.C. 20006
  (202) 783-7000

American Telemarketing Association
  1800 Pickwick Avenue
  Glenview, Illinois 60025
  (312) 724-7700

Association of General Merchandise Chains
  1625 I Street, N.W.
  Washington, D.C. 20006
  (202) 785-2060

Association of Independent Commercial Producers
    100 East 42nd Street
    New York, New York 10017
    (212) 867-5720

Association of National Advertisers
    155 East 44th Street
    New York, New York 10017
    (212) 697-5950

Automotive Advertisers Council
    444 North Michigan Avenue, Suite 2000
    Chicago, Illinois 60611

Bank Marketing Association
    309 West Washington Street
    Chicago, Illinois 60606
    (312) 782-1442

Business/Professional Advertising Association (BPAA)
    205 East 42nd Street
    New York, New York 10017
    (212) 661-0222

Direct Marketing Association
    6 E. 43rd Street
    New York, New York 10017
    (212) 689-4977

Direct Selling Association
    1776 K Street, N.W., Suite 600
    Washington, D.C. 20006
    (202) 293-5760

Institute of Outdoor Advertising
    342 Madison Avenue
    New York, New York 10173
    (212) 986-5920

Intermarket Association of Advertising Agencies
1605 North Main Street
Dayton, Ohio 45405
(513) 279-0681

International Advertising Association
475 5th Avenue
New York, New York 10017
(212) 684-1583

International Association of Business Communicators
870 Market Street, Suite 940
San Francisco, California 84192
(415) 433-3400

International Association of Chain Stores
3800 Moor Place
Alexandria, Virginia 22305
(703) 683-3136

International Chain of Industrial and Technical
     Advertising Agencies
c/o Bozell & Jacobs
2700 U.S. Highway 22
Union, New Jersey 07083
(201) 688-2700

International Federation of Advertising Agencies
1605 Main Street, Suite 1115
Sarasota, Florida 33577
(813) 366-2902

International Marketing Institute
29 Garden Street
Cambridge, Massachusetts 02138
(617) 547-9873

International Public Relations Association,
    U.S. Section
P.O. Box 1001
Little Rock, Arkansas 72203
(501) 372-5231

League of Advertising Agencies
10 West 33rd Street, #PH-A
New York, New York 10001
(212) 967-8089

Life Communicators Association
900 Des Moines Street, Suite 200
Des Moines, Iowa 50309
(515) 266-2189

Mail Advertising Service Association International
7315 Wisconsin Avenue, Suite 440 W.
Bethesda, Maryland 20814
(301) 654-6272

Mail Order Association of America
1877 Bourne Court
Wantagh, New York 11793
(516) 221-8257

Mailing List Users and Suppliers Association
300 Buckelew Avenue
Jamesburg, New Jersey 08831
(201) 521-4441

Marketing Research Association
111 East Wacker Drive, Suite 600
Chicago, Illinois 60601
(312) 644-6610

Marketing Science Institute
1000 Massachusetts Avenue
Cambridge, Massachusetts 02138
(617) 491-2060

Media Research Directors Association
c/o Al Edwards
CBS Magazines
1515 Broadway, 16th Floor
New York, New York 10036
(212) 719-6844

Mutual Advertising Agency Network
8375 East Jefferson Avenue
Detroit, Michigan 48214
(313) 821-0120

National Advertising Agency Network
14 East 48th Street
New York, New York 10017
(212) 355-7230

National Advertising Review Board
845 3rd Avenue
New York, New York 10022
(212) 832-1320

National Association of Advertising Publishers
111 East Wacker Drive, Suite 600
Chicago, Illinois 60601
(312) 644-6610

National Association of Business and Industrial
    Saleswomen
90 Corona, Suite 1407
Denver, Colorado 80218
(303) 777-7257

National Association of Co-op Advertising
    Professionals
145 North Franklin Turnpike
Ramsey, New Jersey 07446
(201) 327-2667

National Association of Market Developers
P.O. Box 4560
Stamford, Connecticut 06907
(203) 329-2926

National Association of Media Women
1185 Niskey Lake Road, S.W.
Atlanta, Georgia 30331
(404) 344-5862

National Association of Professional Saleswomen
P.O. Box 255708
Sacramento, California 95865
(916) 484-1234

National Association of Publishers Reps
114 East 32nd Street, Suite 1406
New York, New York 10016
(212) 683-1836

National Association of Sales and Marketing
    Professionals
c/o Barry Allan
Nelson-Allan
5439 East Charter Oak Road
Scottsdale, Arizona 85254

National Mail Order Association
5818 Venice Boulevard
Los Angeles, California 90019
(213) 934-7986

National Mass Retailing Institute
570 Seventh Avenue
New York, New York 10018
(212) 354-6600

National Network of Women in Sales
P.O. Box 95269
Schaumburg, Illinois 60195
(312) 577-1944

National Premium Sales Executives
1600 Route 22
Union, New Jersey 07083
(201) 687-3090

National Retail Merchants Association
100 West 31st Street
New York, New York 10001
(212) 244-8780

National Society of Sales Training Executives
1040 Woodcock Road
Orlando, Florida 32803
(305) 894-8312

The Networking Institute
Box L-EA
West Newton, Massachusetts 02165
(617) 965-3340

New York/International Association of Business
Communicators
P.O. Box 2025, Grand Central Station
New York, New York 10163
(212) 697-5600

Newspaper Advertising Bureau
1180 Avenue of the Americas
New York, New York 10036
(212) 921-5080

Newspaper Advertising Co-op Network
5105 Tollview Drive
Rolling Meadows, Illinois 60008
(312) 577-8350

Outdoor Advertising Association of America
1899 L Street N.W., Suite 403
Washington, D.C. 20036
(202) 223-5566

Point-of-Purchase Advertising Institute (POPAI)
2 Executive Drive
Fort Lee, New Jersey 07024
(201) 585-8400

Professional Salespersons of America
P.O. Box 10285
100 Maria Circle, N.W.
Albuquerque, New Mexico 87184
(505) 897-4568

Promotion Marketing Association of America
322 Eighth Avenue, Suite 1201
New York, New York 10001
(212) 206-1100

Public Relations Society of America
845 Third Avenue
New York, New York 10022
(212) 826-1750

Public Utilities Communicators Association
c/o Walter K. Conover
122 Decker Drive
New Castle, Pennsylvania 16105
(412) 654-1350

Publishers' Ad Club
c/o Caroline A. Bonett
Denhard & Stewart
122 East 42nd Street
New York, New York 10017
(212) 986-1900

Radio Advertising Bureau
304 Park Avenue South
New York, New York 10010
(212) 254-4800

Retail Advertising Conference
67 East Oak Street
Chicago, Illinois 60611
(312) 280-9344

Sales and Marketing Executives International
6151 Wilson Mills Road, Suite 200
Cleveland, Ohio 44143
(216) 473-2100

Society for Marketing Professional Services
801 North Fairfax Street, Suite 215
Alexandria, Virginia 22314
(703) 549-6117

Specialty Advertising Association International
1404 Walnut Hill Lane
Irving, Texas 75038
(214) 258-0404

Technical Marketing Society of America
   3711 Long Beach Boulevard, Suite 609
   Long Beach, California 90807
   (213) 595-0254

Women Executives in Public Relations
   P.O. Box 781
   Murray Hill Station
   New York, New York 10156
   (212) 683-5438

Women in Advertising and Marketing
   4200 Wisconsin Avenue, N.W., Suite 106-238
   Washington, D.C. 20016
   (301) 279-9093

Women in Sales Association
   8 Madison Avenue
   Valhalla, New York 10595
   (914) 946-3802

Women's Direct Response Group
   P.O. Box 1561, F.D.R. Station
   New York, New York 10150
   (201) 871-1100

CHAPTER 8

REAL MARKETING PEOPLE

In the course of developing this book, we spoke with a number of marketing professionals and asked them questions about their positions, how they got where they are today, and what they would tell someone considering a marketing career. The answers we received were thoughtful, sometimes humorous, but always honest.

We will present a cross-section of marketers, from those just out of school to others well into their careers, in the hope that their various insights will help you in your planning and your decisions. You may notice that many of their opinions reinforce what has been said elsewhere in the book, and we were gratified at the coincidence. Read on, and learn their stories.

SALES REPRESENTATIVE

Nanci Schultz is a sales representative at a large retail-sales terminal distributor. She graduated recently with a B.S. degree in business, concentrating in marketing. With a sales career as a goal, Nanci worked as a manager of a specialty food store where she demonstrated gourmet appliances, and then she worked as a sales representative in a shoe store where she also had advertising responsibility. Naturally, retailing is a good place to begin a sales career, which Nanci's example bears out.

With this background while working her way through college, Nanci was a prime candidate for her current position, which she obtained through on-campus recruiting. After the initial screening, she traveled to Boston for a second full day of interviews with three different district managers. Nanci describes the process as being put in many different selling situations and asked "What would *you* do? How would you handle *this* situation?"

Now a market specialist with the company, Nanci loves her work and sees several opportunities for advancement within her company. In the meantime, she is taking MBA courses at a local university for her own interest, although she does not think the MBA is a must in her field. More important, Nanci maintains, is a "willingness to work hard and an ability to handle rejection."

While you're still in school, do what you can for yourself and become involved in the field, whether on the job or with outside activities like the American Marketing Association. Nanci was a vice-president of programming for the collegiate AMA chapter while in school. She obtained guest speakers and arranged events, which helped her develop and refine some of her selling skills.

Nanci also suggests talking with someone in the field to find out more about a job you're interested in. "Be personable, and get experience," she counsels, again suggesting retail sales as a good place to start. Once on the job, "Take ownership, come up with ideas, and you'll get noticed and have a sense of accomplishment."

In selling, you need to be highly motivated and a self-starter. Nanci stresses the importance of being conscientious and outgoing, but most of all, "have discipline," especially in sales where your time can be discretionary. These are skills you can develop while still in school, and they will serve you well. "Work for yourself," no matter what company you represent, and you'll do the best job you possibly can.

ASSISTANT DIRECTOR OF GRADUATE STUDIES

Susan Macione, assistant to the director of graduate studies at a small northeastern university, is responsible for promoting all executive, co-op, international, and six other masters degrees in business. She develops copy and brochures herself, coordinating with local vendors for production. Photographs used are on file, and artwork is obtained from an on-campus department.

A recent graduate of Western New England College

with a business degree/marketing concentration, Susan was originally a journalism major. Disillusioned with the field, she wanted to build on her communications interests. Writing and advertising especially appealed to her, and an internship at a local department store in the in-house advertising department gave her exposure to many facets of the trade including production and familiarity with different media.

Influenced too by a "dynamite" advertising professor, Susan became involved in advertising research, conducting phone surveys and developing the questionnaires used.

After graduation, Susan worked as manager of an independent computer retail store, where she handled all marketing and advertising, developing brochures and managing all communications for the store. She feels this experience prepared her well for her current position at the university, and her hands-on internship and research experience have provided substance to enhance her education.

From her experience, Susan has learned the importance of knowing the different media and their relationships to a particular target market. In retrospect, Susan wishes she had learned more about this area in school, and she hopes more professors will expand on it in advertising courses.

Susan recommends reading the trade publications in the field to keep up with new developments. She also attends meetings and seminars of the Ad Club and

Women in Communications. Not only does she obtain information, but she has made many personal and professional connections.

When asked what she considered an important skill, Susan replied that organizational ability, being comfortable working with many different people and projects at once, is a major factor in her position. Of course the ability to communicate is taken for granted, but persuasiveness is an additional requirement for an advertiser.

Along those lines, Susan added, "Learn how to market yourself first." She continued to say that getting that first job is "not as easy as you think," but you can get a good idea of what a job or company is like by asking people who are already there. People are generally willing to sit down and talk to you and are pretty receptive to questions. Take advantage of this and find out as much as you can about your prospective field and the employers you are considering. Not only will you come away with an insider's perspective, but you will have practiced some of the skills you will need to use on the job.

PROJECT DIRECTOR

Joe Griffin is project director for a high-tech product at a large communications corporation. Originally intending to become a lawyer, Joe became interested in marketing when he had the opportunity to work for his university's marketing department on an outside consulting job. He worked directly for the researcher in charge of the project, and as a result he obtained his first job after graduation as brand manager for Hart, Schaffner and Marx.

In order to learn more about the field, Joe went on for his MBA at DePaul University while working. To enhance his experience and undergraduate education, Joe studied international business. He saw the need for the American market to expand outside the United States, and he became aware of the emerging electronic technologies being developed worldwide.

Continuing to work in the consumer electronics industry, Joe has held marketing positions at several companies, concentrating on high-ticket and high-technology products. He has marketed just about everything from stereo equipment to cable television to computer shopping. Currently, Joe is working with companies in several countries to develop a worldwide standard in the debit card, the newest development in cashless currency.

As for the traits Joe wants to see in a recent college graduate he would consider hiring, there were several. First, Joe wants to see outside activities that let you practice what you are learning, such as student organizations or marketing-related jobs. He is especially impressed if you have paid for all or part of your education, and if the job provides feedback on how you apply your newly learned skills, so much the better.

Lastly, as advice he gives someone considering a job

like his, Joe recommends taking any position you can to get into the company you want to work for. Once inside, find out where the action—the growth area—is, because they will require people. Companies are likely to look inside at good employees first. Find out about these positions and how your skills can help the company. Often these areas are the riskiest, especially if they involve new products, but they can also be the most rewarding. Also, find someone you respect and are comfortable with, and learn from them. This person does not have to be a mentor, but someone more experienced in the field can be a great help to the novice in any area.

ADVERTISING ACCOUNT EXECUTIVE

Sue Hayes is an account executive with an advertising agency in New York, although she originally intended to go into retailing. After working as an assistant buyer for about six months, Sue returned to college to study "areas of self-interest and exploration": psychology and black studies. Graduating with high honors, she went to work in the social services field for several years, but she found the opportunities for advancement nonexistent and the work depressing. The longer she worked, the more Sue became convinced that marketing was still the field she wanted to enter, but she felt she needed an advanced degree and was willing to go into debt to get it.

As it turned out, Sue received a fellowship and earned her MBA from Columbia University Business School. While there, she accepted a summer internship with a large communications company. She wrote the situation analysis of the project coinciding with the company's interest in targeting the black consumer market, which was only beginning to be of interest as a target group. This internship became a full-time job upon graduation, and she became manager of the mature market and handled several projects for this segment.

Seeing an opportunity to work much closer to home at a substantial salary increase, Sue accepted an offer from an advertising agency. In this position, Sue is responsible for a liquor account, a personal care client, and a communications company. Incidentally, Sue considers advertising experience a necessity for a well-rounded marketing career and highly recommends it to serious students of marketing.

When assessing a potential employee, Sue looks for "intelligence, energy, and sincerity"; she is willing to look at a candidate's entire background and not just business degrees. She also looks for someone who "wants to be doing the job, who is eager, aggressive, and willing to learn and take direction." She does want to see extracurricular activity of some kind, some indication of leadership or initiative, including working to put oneself through school. Then perhaps dean's list or other honors to round out the background—Sue wants to see some balance, not only academic accomplishment.

"Have *good* communication skills," Sue stressed. "Presentation skills are especially important—the ability to present and defend your position is so important in any facet of marketing, or in business for that matter. How many times will you be called on to propose a new idea or justify another study?" Good places to learn are available in debating clubs, acting, speech and theater courses, and student council.

Sue also encourages students to be aggressive about calling people to ask about jobs or schools of interest. This is a great way to dispel illusions and make your expectations more realistic. It is also a great way to meet people, and because it shows initiative, you may even receive job offers.

MARKETING COMMUNICATIONS MANAGER

Jerry Orenstein is the manager of marketing communications for consumer products at a large durable-goods company headquartered in Japan. With a dual undergraduate major in marketing and chemistry from Purdue University, Jerry was greatly influenced by Dr. Perloff, onetime president of the American Psychological Association. As a result, Jerry went on to concentrate in consumer psychology while earning his MBA from the City University of New York.

Jerry spent the first seven years of his career in advertising and market research, learning how to conduct research, test communications, and evaluate one's own product. The next step on the career ladder was overseas for General Motors to look at the international market, again analyzing the appropriateness of the product and the effectiveness of the communications. Back home in the United States, Jerry went to GAF Corporation as director of research and communications, responsible for all aspects of research and communications for consumer products. Then he moved to U.S. Pioneer Corporation, the American distributor of consumer electronic products for the Japanese parent company. Jerry served as manager of marketing services, where again he was in charge of all communications functions. Coleco was the next beneficiary of Jerry's skills, where he was involved in the development and launching of video games, Colecovision, and of course the Cabbage Patch Kid.

Throughout his career, Jerry's focus has remained fixed on communication and its place in marketing. Ideally, he says he would like to "take market research one step further and input communications aspects." Too many companies are product-driven, he claims. They manufacture an item and leave it to marketing to create demand for it. As we already know, this does not work. On the other hand, the proper use of research could tell the manufacturer what the public would like to buy, and this is the element Jerry is most interested in. We look forward to seeing his contributions to the field of market research.

When asked what he looks for in a potential employee, Jerry replies, "Someone who is willing to learn and is not salary-oriented. Too many people come out of college expecting exorbitant pay, and they don't have any experience. You have to change your attitude and pay your dues up front. Start from the bottom and *learn*, no matter what school you went to." He also likes to see some related experience, such as a summer internship or active membership in the collegiate chapter of the American Marketing Association.

Jerry also recommends taking as many computer courses as possible and going on for your MBA directly. He says "You need the MBA. It's hard enough to get ahead. Do it while you're working. This way you get the experience you need as well as the degree. Since many employers provide tuition assistance, take advantage of it." For a few years you'll be very busy, but it will pay off in the long run with a more rewarding career.

To keep up to date with the latest developments in his field, this marketing executive listens to speeches and reads newsletters at his association's information center. (Point of Purchase Advertising Institute photo)

CHAPTER 9

MARKET YOURSELF

Now that you've learned about marketing in general, it's time to apply some marketing techniques to yourself—the college applicant or job seeker. Yes, the four P's can be put to work by you and for you, so just sit back and we'll tell you how.

YOUR PRODUCT

First, think of yourself as a product (the first "P"). Who are your customers? Aren't they the people who will be judging your entrance essay or your résumé? Of course they are, and like any good marketer your first step is to get to know them (personally or not) and find out what it is they want in this kind of product—a student or employee. Look at some of the comments made by the marketers in the previous chapter for some ideas of what makes a job applicant look promising. Talk to people who are now students at the school you would like to attend, and ask them what kind of person fits in

87

best. You may find out in the process that a particular school or job is not right for you, but that is one of the purposes of this exercise.

As you learn about what employers look for, think about what you are looking for in an employer and how the two might or might not fit together. This goes for schools, too, as what one student likes about the diversity of a large university, for example, another may find distracting or confusing. Do some market research, and dig up all you can about your target customer.

If you are looking for a job in a particular field, you can check the *Business Periodicals Index* for articles relating to that field, as well as articles on specific companies. The *National Newspaper Index* is another good source of recent information, and the trade journals of any given field will give you even greater depth.

For an overall financial picture, the 10K published by the Securities Exchange Commission is invaluable and should be used as a balance to the annual report put out by the company. This kind of research is called "doing your homework" for an interview, and it will help you speak intelligently to a recruiter or personnel representative. By taking the time and effort to do this research, you demonstrate your interest in a field and company in addition to your commitment to obtaining meaningful and rewarding work.

YOUR PRICE

The price, of course, is your salary. Naturally you want the highest you can obtain, but isn't there more to rewarding work than just money? Take this into account as you weigh different opportunities. Don't overlook the experience you might gain as part of the compensation for a career position.

YOUR PLACE

You must also be in the right *place* at the right time. Only you have your unique set of skills, and one of these skills is convincing a potential employer that you are the one right person for that job. They need someone like you right now, and here you are!

YOUR PROMOTION

Promotion is the fourth "P." You are sending out résumés, following up, talking to anyone and everyone, establishing contacts, making connections, all with your potential customers. Doesn't that qualify as self-promotion? Of course it does, and it works very well indeed. You obtained professional assistance with your résumé and cover letter and learned how to best present your prior experience, your academic credentials, and your career objectives. Now that your paper self is professional, what about your personal self? We hope we don't need to remind you to dress neatly and conservatively for your interview. That does not mean you must run out and buy a three-piece navy suit, but your interview attire should not be too far from it. Suits are still the overwhelming favorite, and it's hard to go wrong with one. Remember, you will be judged by the appearance you present, and first impressions are the ones that will be remembered most. Take advantage of this and put your best foot (shoes shined!) forward. Not only will you look better, you'll feel better—more comfortable and confident. Even though you may be wearing a suit and tie, your comfort will be based on being appropriately and professionally dressed.

INTERVIEW QUESTIONS AND
SELF-ASSESSMENT

This is a collection of some of the most frequently used questions on job interviews. You can develop your answers to these in the course of analyzing your career goals and your professional needs. Use these questions as a guide to your self-analysis, and compare your answers throughout the course of your career (academic, business, or both).

What are your long-range career objectives? In other words, what are you looking for from a career besides the obvious ability to pay the bills?

How do you plan to accomplish these objectives? What

are you doing to work toward your goals? Are you continuing your education or applying yourself whole-heartedly to your current position?

Why did you select this career? Are you really committed to this line of business or did it just sound glamorous? Is it really for you?

What do you see yourself doing in five years? In ten years? A corollary to your long-range career goals, but with specific deadlines.

What nonoccupational goals have you set for yourself over the next ten years? What is your personal agenda? (You do have a life outside of work, don't you?)

What do you really want to do in life? Be careful, if the answer is not the career in which you are applying for entry, then something is amiss and needs attention.

What are the most important rewards you expect from your business career? Is money the only thing you want from a job? There are other paybacks that are frequently more satisfying.

What salary do you think you will earn in five years? How realistic are your goals? How ambitious are you?

Which is more important to you, the kind of work or the salary? Again, how money-oriented are you? Your employer does want a well-rounded worker, one who seeks satisfaction in doing a good job.

How has your college experience prepared you for a career in business? What did you learn besides your academic area? Did you gain any interpersonal and communication skills or were you a loner?

What qualifications do you have that you think will make you successful in business? Are you organized, a team player, a good communicator, a leader?

What does the word success *mean to you?* Is it large salary, corporate power, expensive car, or does it say job satisfaction?

What do you think it takes to be successful in this kind of company? Do you expect ruthless competitiveness or the cooperation of working toward a common goal?

How do you think you can contribute to our company? What skills and attitude do you have? Will you be a thoughtful, productive team member?

Why should I hire you? This is a biggie. Of course, you would be the perfect employee, this job has your name on it. Emphasize your skills, and turn your weaknesses into learning opportunities.

How would you describe yourself? A few, very few, well-chosen words, like intelligent, curious, cooperative—you get the idea.

How do you think a friend or professor who knows you

well would describe you? Again, only a few words are necessary. Industrious, diligent, etc.

What motivates you to work your hardest? What makes you really tick, and is it something the company does already? Or are you going to be someone the company has to light a fire under?

What accomplishments have given you the most satisfaction? Why? The answer to this question yields several clues to what you've done, as well as what you like to do.

What was your most rewarding experience in college? How did you utilize your college years to gain the most from them? Was it the night you outdrank your buddies or the night you received a community service award?

Why did you choose the school you attended? How selective were you? How choosy was the school? Did you take an active part?

How did you select your major? How well-researched was your decision? Again, did you take an active role?

What subjects did you enjoy most? Why? Of course, your major should be high on this list, but what about others outside your discipline? You are well-rounded, aren't you?

If you could do it again, what would you change in your college studies? Ah, the famous hindsight question, which demands a thoughtful, insightful answer. Do not treat this one lightly.

What changes would you make in your college? Given the chance, how would you improve your school academically?

Do you plan to continue your education? What kind of degree would you pursue? How does it relate to your career? Indicate some consideration of an advanced degree or additional training.

What did you learn from participating in extracurricular activities? How did you develop personally? Can you work with or lead others?

If you were looking for someone to fill this position, what kind of person would you hire? Someone just like yourself, of course—bright, articulate, well-versed in the field.

How are you evaluating companies you might like to work for? Hopefully not just by salary or proximity to the beach. Opportunity for advancement and professional growth should rate high on the list.

What made you decide to apply to this company? Not only professional opportunities, but the company's reputation as a leader in its field, certainly.

In what kind of work are you most at home? Are you quantitatively oriented and happy with numbers, or do figures make you run the other way but you're terrific with people?

Describe your ideal job. Challenging, naturally, but in what way? Opportunity for growth and advancement should also figure in this answer.

How do you work under pressure? Are you cool, calm, and collected, or do you yell at people but still get the job done? Should you consider another line of work?

What qualities do you think make a good manager? This is really asking about what kinds of people you work best with—with whom are you most compatible?

What kind of manager/subordinate relationship do you think works best? What has your interpersonal experience been and will it fit in our company?

What size company do you want to work for? This also relates to your interpersonal style and experience, along with the organizational differences between large and small companies. What are your reasons behind your preference?

How do you analyze potential employers? Are you looking for a large, well-established organization with a deeply entrenched political structure, or are you entrepreneurial and a risk taker, looking for a more flexible structure?

Why did you leave a previous job? Of course it was for

professional advancement, wasn't it? A better opportunity?

Will you relocate? Do you prefer a specific geographical area? Why? Will you travel? How flexible are you, and how much do you want that promotion? In some organizations mobility is the key to advancement, and willingness is taken for granted.

What have you learned from mistakes? How have you turned blunders into learning opportunities? Or are you going to continue to make the same errors over and over?

Are you a perfectionist? A favorite loaded question, this one requires a careful answer. If you say "yes," do you mean you cannot tolerate your coworkers' humanity? If you say "no," does it indicate lower standards for your own work? Watch this one!

We've just about exhausted popular interview territory. Take a few minutes every so often to review these questions and develop your answers. Not only will you be better prepared for the interview, but you will have gained insight to your own career requirements.

COLLEGES WITH MAJORS IN MARKETING

The following four-year colleges offer majors in marketing. For more information, address your correspondence to the department of marketing of each school in which you are interested.

BACHELOR'S DEGREE

Alabama

Alabama Agricultural and Mechanical University
Normal, AL 35762

Alabama State University
Montgomery, AL 36195

Auburn University
Auburn University, AL 36849

Huntingdon College
Montgomery, AL 36194

Jacksonville State University
Jacksonville, AL 36265

Judson College
  Marion, AL 36756

Samford University
  Birmingham, AL 35229

Troy State University, Troy
  Troy, AL 36081

Tuskegee University
  Tuskegee Institute, AL 36088

University of Alabama, Birmingham
  Birmingham, AL 35294

University of Alabama, Huntsville
  Huntsville, AL 35899

University of Alabama, University
  University, AL 35486

University of Montevallo
  Montevallo, AL 35115

University of North Alabama
  Florence, AL 35632

University of South Alabama
  Mobile, AL 36688

Alaska

University of Alaska, Anchorage
  Anchorage, AK 99508

Arizona

Arizona State University
  Tempe, AZ 85281

Northern Arizona University
  Flagstaff, AZ 86011

University of Arizona
  Tucson, AZ 85721

Arkansas

Arkansas State University, State University
  State University, AR 72467

College of the Ozarks
  Clarksville, AR 72830

Harding University
  Searcy, AR 72143

Southern Arkansas University, Magnolia
  Magnolia, AR 71753

University of Arkansas, Fayetteville
  Fayetteville, AR 72701

University of Arkansas, Little Rock
  Little Rock, AR 72204

University of Arkansas, Monticello
  Monticello, AR 71655

University of Central Arkansas
  Conway, AR 72032

California

Armstrong University
  Berkeley, CA 94704

California State College, Bakersfield
  Bakersfield, CA 93309

California State Polytech University, Pomona
  Pomona, CA 91768

California State University, Dominguez Hills
  Carson, CA 90747

California State University, Long Beach
Long Beach, CA 90840

California State University, Los Angeles
Los Angeles, CA 90032

California State University, Northridge
Northridge, CA 91330

California State University, Sacramento
Sacramento, CA 95819

California State University, Stanislaus
Turlock, CA 95380

Golden Gate University
San Francisco, CA 94105

National University
San Diego, CA 92108

Pacific Union College
Angwin, CA 94508

San Diego State University
San Diego, CA 92182

San Francisco State University
San Francisco, CA 94132

San Jose State University
San Jose, CA 95192

Santa Clara University
Santa Clara, CA 95053

University of La Verne
La Verne, CA 91750

University of San Francisco
San Francisco, CA 94177

Woodbury University
  Los Angeles, CA 90017

Colorado

Adams State College
  Alamosa, CO 81102

Colorado State University
  Fort Collins, CO 80523

Metropolitan State College
  Denver, CO 80204

University of Colorado, Boulder
  Boulder, CO 80309

University of Colorado, Colorado Springs
  Colorado Springs, CO 80933

University of Colorado, Denver
  Denver, CO 80202

University of Denver
  Denver, CO 80208

University of Northern Colorado
  Greeley, CO 80639

Connecticut

Central Connecticut State University
  New Britain, CT 06050

Eastern Connecticut State University
  Willimantic, CT 06226

Post College
  Waterbury, CT 06708

Quinnipiac College
  Hamden, CT 06518

University of Bridgeport
  Bridgeport, CT 06601

University of Connecticut, Storrs
  Storrs, CT 06268

University of Hartford
  West Hartford, CT 06117

University of New Haven
  West Haven, CT 06516

Western Connecticut State University
  Danbury, CT 06810

Delaware

Goldey Beacom College
  Wilmington, DE 19808

University of Delaware
  Newark, DE 19716

District of Columbia

American University
  Washington, DC 20016

Georgetown University
  Washington, DC 20057

George Washington University
  Washington, DC 20052

Howard University
  Washington, DC 20059

Mount Vernon College
  Washington, DC 20007

Southeastern University
Washington, DC 20024

Florida

Barry University
Miami, FL 33161

Bethune-Cookman College
Daytona Beach, FL 32015

College of Boca Raton
Boca Raton, FL 33431

Florida Agriculture and Mechanical University
Tallahassee, FL 32307

Florida Atlantic University
Boca Raton, FL 33431

Florida Institute of Technology
Melbourne, FL 32901

Florida International University
Miami, FL 33199

Florida State University
Tallahassee, FL 32306

Fort Lauderdale College
Fort Lauderdale, FL 33301

Jacksonville University
Jacksonville, FL 32211

Jones College, Jacksonville
Jacksonville, FL 32211

Orlando College
Orlando, FL 32810

St. Thomas University
Miami, FL 33054

Stetson University
  Deland, FL 32720

University of Central Florida
  Orlando, FL 32816

University of Florida
  Gainesville, FL 32611

University of North Florida
  Jacksonville, FL 32216

University of South Florida
  Tampa, FL 33620

University of Tampa
  Tampa, FL 33606

University of West Florida
  Pensacola, FL 32504

Webber College
  Babson Park, FL 33827

Georgia

Atlanta University
  Atlanta, GA 30314

Augusta College
  Augusta, GA 30910

Columbus College
  Columbus, GA 31907

Fort Valley State College
  Fort Valley, GA 31030

Georgia College
  Milledgeville, GA 31061

Georgia Southern College
  Statesboro, GA 30460

Georgia Southwestern College
Americus, GA 31709

Georgia State University
Atlanta, GA 30303

Kennesaw College
Marietta, GA 30061

Mercer University, Atlanta
Atlanta, GA 30341

Savannah State College
Savannah, GA 31404

University of Georgia
Athens, GA 30602

Valdosta State College
Valdosta, GA 31698

West Georgia College
Carrollton, GA 30118

Hawaii

Chaminade University of Honolulu
Honolulu, HI 96816

University of Hawaii, Manoa
Honolulu, HI 96822

Idaho

Boise State University
Boise, ID 83725

College of Idaho
Caldwell, ID 83605

Idaho State University
Pocatello, ID 83209

University of Idaho
  Moscow, ID 83843

Illinois

Aurora University
  Aurora, IL 60506

Bradley University
  Peoria, IL 61625

Chicago State University
  Chicago, IL 60628

DePaul University
  Chicago, IL 60604

Eastern Illinois University
  Charleston, IL 61920

Elmhurst College
  Elmhurst, IL 60126

Eureka College
  Eureka, IL 61530

Greenville College
  Greenville, IL 62246

Illinois State University
  Normal, IL 61761

Lewis University
  Romeoville, IL 60441

Loyola University of Chicago
  Chicago, IL 60611

MacMurray College
  Jacksonville, IL 62650

McKendree College
  Lebanon, IL 62254

Millikin University
  Decatur, IL 62522

Mundelein College
  Chicago, IL 60660

Northeastern Illinois University
  Chicago, IL 60625

Northern Illinois University
  DeKalb, IL 60115

Quincy College
  Quincy, IL 62301

Roosevelt University
  Chicago, IL 60605

Southern Illinois University, Carbondale
  Carbondale, IL 62901

Trinity Christian College
  Palos Heights, IL 60463

University of Illinois at Chicago
  Chicago, IL 60680

Western Illinois University
  Macomb, IL 61455

Indiana

Indiana Central University
  Indianapolis, IN 46227

Indiana State University, Terre Haute
  Terre Haute, IN 47809

Indiana University-Purdue University, Fort Wayne
  Fort Wayne, IN 46805

Indiana University, South Bend
  South Bend, IN 46634

Manchester College
  North Manchester, IN 46962

Martin Central College
  Indianapolis, IN 46205

Purdue University, Calumet
  Hammond, IN 46323

St. Joseph's College
  Rensselaer, IN 47978

St. Mary-of-the-Woods College
  St Mary/Wood, IN 47876

Tri-State University
  Angola, IN 46703

University of Evansville
  Evansville, IN 47702

University of Notre Dame
  Notre Dame, IN 46556

University of Southern Indiana
  Evansville, IN 47712

Iowa

Drake University
  Des Moines, IA 50311

Iowa State University
  Ames, IA 50011

Loras College
  Dubuque, IA 52001

University of Iowa
  Iowa City, IA 52242

University of Northern Iowa
  Cedar Falls, IA 50613

Upper Iowa University
Fayette, IA 52142

Westmar College
Lemars, IA 51031

Kansas

Emporia State University
Emporia, KS 66801

Fort Hays State University
Hays, KS 67601

Kansas Newman College
Wichita, KS 67213

Kansas State University
Manhattan, KS 66506

Pittsburg State University
Pittsburg, KS 66762

Washburn University of Topeka
Topeka, KS 66621

Wichita State University
Wichita, KS 67208

Kentucky

Eastern Kentucky University
Richmond, KY 40475

Kentucky State University
Frankfort, KY 40601

Morehead State University
Morehead, KY 40351

Murray State University
Murray, KY 42071

Northern Kentucky University
  Highland Heights, KY 41076

University of Kentucky
  Lexington, KY 40506

University of Louisville
  Louisville, KY 40292

Western Kentucky University
  Bowling Green, KY 42101

Louisiana

Grambling State University
  Grambling, LA 71245

Louisiana State University, Baton Rouge
  Baton Rouge, LA 70803

Louisiana State University, Shreveport
  Shreveport, LA 71115

Louisiana Tech University
  Ruston, LA 71272

Loyola University
  New Orleans, LA 70118

McNeese State University
  Lake Charles, LA 70609

Nicholls State University
  Thibodaux, LA 70310

Northeast Louisiana University
  Monroe, LA 71209

Southeastern Louisiana University
  Hammond, LA 70402

University of New Orleans
  New Orleans, LA 70148

University of Southwestern Louisiana
Lafayette, LA 70501

Xavier University of Louisiana
New Orleans, LA 70125

Maine

Husson College
Bangor, ME 04401

Thomas College
Waterville, ME 04901

University of Maine, Machias
Machias, ME 04654

University of Maine, Orono
Orono, ME 04469

Maryland

Loyola College
Baltimore, MD 21210

Morgan State University
Baltimore, MD 21239

University of Baltimore
Baltimore, MD 21201

University of Maryland, College Park
College Park, MD 20742

Massachusetts

American International College
Springfield, MA 01109

Anna Maria College for Men and Women
Paxton, MA 01612

Babson College
  Babson Park, MA 02157

Bentley College
  Waltham, MA 02154

Boston College
  Chestnut Hill, MA 02167

Fitchburg State College
  Fitchburg, MA 01420

Merrimack College
  North Andover, MA 01845

Nichols College
  Dudley, MA 01570

Northeastern University
  Boston, MA 02115

Salem State College
  Salem, MA 01970

Simmons College
  Boston, MA 02115

Southeastern Massachusetts University
  North Dartmouth, MA 02747

Stonehill College
  North Easton, MA 02356

Suffolk University
  Boston, MA 02114

University of Massachusetts, Amherst
  Amherst, MA 01003

Western New England College
Springfield, MA 01119

Michigan

Andrews University
Berrien Springs, MI 49104

Central Michigan University
Mount Pleasant, MI 48859

Davenport College
Grand Rapids, MI 49503

Detroit College of Business
Dearborn, MI 48126

Eastern Michigan University
Ypsilanti, MI 48197

Ferris State College
Big Rapids, MI 49307

Grand Valley State College
Allendale, MI 49401

Lawrence Institute of Technology
Southfield, MI 48075

Madonna College
Livonia, MI 48150

Marygrove College
Detroit, MI 48221

Mercy College of Detroit
Detroit, MI 48219

Michigan State University
Easter Lansing, MI 48824

Michigan Tech University
Houghton, MI 49931

Northern Michigan University
  Marquette, MI 49855

Northwood Institute
  Midland, MI 48640

Oakland University
  Rochester, MI 48063

Olivet College
  Olivet, MI 49076

Saginaw Valley State College
  University Center, MI 48710

University of Detroit
  Detroit, MI 48221

University of Michigan, Flint
  Flint, MI 48503

Wayne State University
  Detroit, MI 48202

Western Michigan University
  Kalamazoo, MI 49008

Minnesota

College of St. Catherine
  St. Paul, MN 55105

College of St. Thomas
  St. Paul, MN 55105

Mankato State University
  Mankato, MN 56001

Moorhead State University
  Moorhead, MN 56560

Northwestern College
  Roseville, MN 55113

St. Cloud State University
  St. Cloud, MN 56301

St. Mary's College
  Winona, MN 55987

Southwest State University
  Marshall, MN 56258

University of Minnesota, Duluth
  Duluth, MN 55812

Mississippi

Delta State University
  Cleveland, MS 38733

Jackson State University
  Jackson, MS 39217

Mississippi State University
  Mississippi State, MS 39762

University of Mississippi, University
  University, MS 38677

University of Southern Mississippi
  Hattiesburg, MS 39401

Missouri

Avila College
  Kansas City, MO 64145

Central Missouri State University
  Warrensburg, MO 64093

Clayton University
  Clayton, MO 63105

Columbia College
  Columbia, MO 65216

Fontbonne College
  St. Louis, MO 63105

Lincoln University
  Jefferson City, MO 65101

Missouri Southern State College
  Joplin, MO 64801

Missouri Western State College
  St. Joseph, MO 64507

Northeast Missouri State University
  Kirksville, MO 63501

Northwest Missouri State University
  Maryville, MO 64468

Rockhurst College
  Kansas City, MO 64110

St. Louis University
  St. Louis, MO 63103

Southeast Missouri State University
  Cape Girardeau, MO 63701

Southwest Missouri State University
  Springfield, MO 65804

Webster University
  Webster Groves, MO 63119

William Woods College
  Fulton, MO 65251

Montana

Eastern Montana College
  Billings, MT 59101

Montana State University
Bozeman, MT 59717

Nebraska

Chadron State College
Chadron, NE 69337

College of St. Mary
Omaha, NE 68124

Creighton University
Omaha, NE 68178

Kearney State College
Kearney, NE 68849

Midland Lutheran College
Fremont, NE 68025

University of Nebraska, Lincoln
Lincoln, NE 68588

University of Nebraska, Omaha
Omaha, NE 68182

Nevada

University of Nevada, Las Vegas
Las Vegas, NV 89154

University of Nevada, Reno
Reno, NV 89557

New Hampshire

Franklin Pierce College
Rindge, NH 03461

New England College
Henniker, NH 03242

New Hampshire College
Manchester, NH 03104

Plymouth State College of the University of New Hampshire
Plymouth, NH 03264

Rivier College
Nashua, NH 03060

New Jersey

Centenary College
Hackettstown, NJ 07840

Fairleigh Dickinson University, Florham-Madison
Madison, NJ 07940

Fairleigh Dickinson University, Rutherford
Rutherford, NJ 07070

Fairleigh Dickinson University, Teaneck-Hackensack
Teaneck, NJ 07666

Monmouth College
West Long Branch, NJ 07764

Montclair State College
Upper Montclair, NJ 07043

Rider College
Lawrenceville, NJ 08648

Rutgers State University of New Jersey, Newark
Newark, NJ 07102

Rutgers State University of New Jersey, New Brunswick
New Brunswick, NJ 08903

St. Peter's College
Jersey City, NJ 07306

Seton Hall University
South Orange, NJ 07079

Thomas A. Edison State College
  Trenton, NJ 08625

Trenton State College
  Trenton, NJ 08625

New Mexico

New Mexico State University, Las Cruces
  Las Cruces, NM 88003

University of New Mexico, Albuquerque
  Albuquerque, NM 87131

Western New Mexico University
  Silver City, NM 88061

New York

Alfred University
  Alfred, NY 14802

Baruch College
  New York, NY 10010

Canisius College
  Buffalo, NY 14208

C.W. Post College
  Greenvale, NY 11548

Daemen College
  Amherst, NY 14226

Dowling College
  Oakdale, NY 11769

Hofstra University
  Hempstead, NY 11550

Iona College
  New Rochelle, NY 10801

Ithaca College
Ithaca, NY 14850

Long Island University, Brooklyn Center
Brooklyn, NY 11201

Manhattan College
Riverdale, NY 10471

New York Institute of Technology, Old Westbury
Old Westbury, NY 11568

New York University
New York, NY 10003

Niagara University
Niagara University, NY 14109

Pace University, New York
New York, NY 10038

Pace University, Pleasantville/Briarcliff
Pleasantville, NY 10570

Pace University, White Plains
White Plains, NY 10603

Rochester Institute of Technology
Rochester, NY 14623

Russell Sage College
Troy, NY 12180

St. Bonaventure University
St. Bonaventure, NY 14778

St. John's University
Jamaica, NY 11439

St. Thomas Aquinas College
Sparkill, NY 10976

Siena College
Loudonville, NY 12211

State University of New York, College of Plattsburgh
  Plattsburgh, NY 12901

Syracuse University
  Syracuse, NY 13210

University of the State of New York, Regents College Degrees
  Albany, NY 12230

Wagner College
  Staten Island, NY 10301

York College
  Jamaica, NY 11451

North Carolina

Appalachian State University
  Boone, NC 28608

Campbell University
  Buies Creek, NC 27506

East Carolina University
  Greenville, NC 27834

University of North Carolina, Greensboro
  Greensboro, NC 27412

University of North Carolina, Wilmington
  Wilmington, NC 28403

Western Carolina University
  Cullowhee, NC 28723

North Dakota

University of North Dakota, Grand Forks
  Grand Forks, ND 58202

Ohio

Ashland College
  Ashland, OH 44805

Baldwin-Wallace College
  Berea, OH 44017

Central State University
  Wilberforce, OH 45384

Cleveland State University
  Cleveland, OH 44115

Defiance College
  Defiance, OH 43512

Dyke College
  Cleveland, OH 44115

Findlay College
  Findlay, OH 45840

Franklin University
  Columbus, OH 43215

John Carroll University
  Cleveland, OH 44118

Lake Erie College
  Painesville, OH 44077

Marietta College
  Marietta, OH 45750

Miami University, Oxford
  Oxford, OH 45056

Ohio Northern University
  Ada, OH 45810

Ohio University, Athens
  Athens, OH 45701

Rio Grande College
Rio Grande, OH 45674

University of Akron
Akron, OH 44325

University of Dayton
Dayton, OH 45469

University of Toledo
Toledo, OH 43606

Wilberforce University
Wilberforce, OH 45384

Wright State University, Dayton
Dayton, OH 45435

Xavier University
Cincinnati, OH 45207

Youngstown State University
Youngstown, OH 44555

Oklahoma

Bethany Nazarene College
Bethany, OK 73008

Central State University
Edmond, OK 73034

Northeastern Oklahoma State University
Tahlequah, OK 74464

Oklahoma Baptist University
Shawnee, OK 74801

Oklahoma Christian College
Oklahoma City, OK 73111

Oklahoma City University
Oklahoma City, OK 73106

Oklahoma State University
  Stillwater, OK 74078

Oral Roberts University
  Tulsa, OK 74171

Phillips University
  Enid, OK 73701

Southwestern Oklahoma State University
  Weatherford, OK 73096

University of Oklahoma, Norman
  Norman, OK 73019

University of Tulsa
  Tulsa, OK 74104

Oregon

Portland State University
  Portland, OR 97207

University of Oregon, Eugene
  Eugene, OR 97403

University of Portland
  Portland, OR 97203

Pennsylvania

Beaver College
  Glenside, PA 19038

Cabrini College
  Radnor, PA 19087

Chestnut Hill College
  Philadelphia, PA 19118

Clarion University of Pennsylvania
  Clarion, PA 16214

Duquesne University
  Pittsburgh, PA 15282

Elizabethtown College
  Elizabethtown, PA 17022

Gannon University
  Erie, PA 16501

Holy Family College
  Philadelphia, PA 19114

Indiana University of Pennsylvania
  Indiana, PA 15705

King's College
  Wilkes-Barre, PA 18711

Kutztown University
  Kutztown, PA 19530

La Salle University
  Philadelphia, PA 19141

Lehigh University
  Bethlehem, PA 18015

Messiah College
  Grantham PA 17027

Pennsylvania State University, Capitol
  Middletown, PA 17057

Pennsylvania State University, University Park
  University Park, PA 16802

Philadelphia College of Textiles and Science
  Philadelphia, PA 19144

Robert Morris College
  Coraopolis, PA 15108

St. Joseph's University
  Philadelphia, PA 19131

Slippery Rock University
  Slippery Rock, PA 16057

Susquehanna University
  Selinsgrove, PA 17870

Temple University
  Philadelphia, PA 19122

University of Pennsylvania
  Philadelphia, PA 19104

University of Scranton
  Scranton, PA 18510

Villanova University
  Villanova, PA 19085

Waynesburg College
  Waynesburg, PA 15370

York College of Pennsylvania
  York, PA 17405

Rhode Island

Bryant College
  Smithfield, RI 02917

Johnson & Wales College
  Providence, RI 02903

Providence College
  Providence, RI 02918

Roger Williams College, Bristol
  Bristol, RI 02809

University of Rhode Island
Kingston, RI 02881

South Carolina

Baptist College, Charleston
Charleston, SC 29411

Benedict College
Columbia, SC 29204

Claflin College
Orangeburg, SC 29115

Coker College
Hartsville, SC 29550

South Carolina State College
Orangeburg, SC 29117

University of South Carolina, Coastal Carolina College
Conway, SC 29526

University of South Carolina, Spartanburg
Spartanburg, SC 29303

South Dakota

Northern State College
Aberdeen, SD 57401

Tennessee

Belmont College
Nashville, TN 37203

Christian Brothers College
Memphis, TN 38104

David Lipscomb College
Nashville, TN 37203

East Tennessee State University
  Johnson City, TN 37614

Freed-Hardeman College
  Henderson, TN 38340

Lambuth College
  Jackson, TN 38301

Lincoln Memorial University
  Harrogate, TN 37752

Memphis State University
  Memphis, TN 38152

Middle Tennessee State University
  Murfreesboro, TN 37132

Tennessee Tech University
  Cookeville, TN 38501

Union University
  Jackson, TN 38305

University of Tennessee, Knoxville
  Knoxville, TN 37996

University of Tennessee, Martin
  Martin, TN 38238

Texas

Abilene Christian University
  Abilene, TX 79699

Amber University
  Garland, TX 75041

Angelo State University
  San Angelo, TX 76909

Baylor University
  Waco, TX 76798

Corpus Christi State University
Corpus Christi, TX 78412

Dallas Baptist University
Dallas, TX 75211

East Texas State University, Commerce
Commerce, TX 75428

East Texas State University, Texarkana
Texarkana, TX 75501

Hardin-Simmons University
Abilene, TX 79698

Houston Baptist University
Houston, TX 77074

Howard Payne University
Brownwood, TX 76801

Huston-Tillotson College
Austin, TX 78702

Incarnate Word College
San Antonio, TX 78209

Lamar University, Beaumont
Beaumont, TX 77710

Midwestern State University
Wichita Falls, TX 76308

North Texas State University
Denton, TX 76203

Pan American University
Edinburg, TX 78539

Prairie View A & M University
Prairie View, TX 77446

St. Mary's University of San Antonio
San Antonio, TX 78284

Sam Houston State University
  Huntsville, TX 77341

Southern Methodist University
  Dallas, TX 75275

Southwest Texas State University
  San Marcos, TX 78666

Stephen F. Austin State University
  Nacogdoches, TX 75962

Sul Ross State University
  Alpine, TX 79830

Tarleton State University
  Stephenville, TX 76402

Texas A & M University, College Station
  College Station, TX 77843

Texas Christian University
  Fort Worth, TX 76129

Texas Lutheran College
  Seguin, TX 78155

Texas Tech University
  Lubbock, TX 79409

Texas Wesleyan College
  Fort Worth, TX 76105

Texas Woman's University
  Denton, TX 76204

University of Houston, University Park
  Houston, TX 77004

University of Mary Hardin-Baylor
  Belton, TX 76513

University of Texas, Arlington
  Arlington, TX 76019

University of Texas, Austin
  Austin, TX 78712

University of Texas, El Paso
  El Paso, TX 79968

University of Texas of the Permian Basin
  Odessa, TX 79762

University of Texas, San Antonio
  San Antonio, TX 78285

University of Texas, Tyler
  Tyler, TX 75701

Wayland Baptist University
  Plainview, TX 79072

West Texas State University
  Canyon, TX 79016

Utah

University of Utah
  Salt Lake City, UT 84112

Utah State University
  Logan, UT 84322

Weber State College
  Ogden, UT 84408

Westminster College of Salt Lake City
  Salt Lake City, UT 84105

Vermont

Castleton State College
  Castleton, VT 05735

Green Mountain College
  Poultney, VT 05764

University of Vermont
  Burlington, VT 05405

Virginia

Averett College
  Danville, VA 24541

George Mason University
  Fairfax, VA 22030

Hampton University
  Hampton, VA 23668

James Madison University
  Harrisonburg, VA 22807

Marymount College of Virginia
  Arlington, VA 22207

Old Dominion University
  Norfolk, VA 23508

Virginia Commonwealth University
  Richmond, VA 23284

Virginia Polytechnical Institute and State University
  Blacksburg, VA 24061

Washington

Eastern Washington University
  Cheney, WA 99004

Gonzaga University
  Spokane, WA 99258

Pacific Lutheran University
  Tacoma, WA 98447

Seattle Pacific University
  Seattle, WA 98119

Seattle University
Seattle, WA 98122

West Virginia

Bluefield State College
Bluefield, WV 24701

Concord College
Athens, WV 24712

Davis & Elkins College
Elkins, WV 26241

Marshall University
Huntington, WV 25701

Salem College, Salem
Salem, WV 26426

Shepherd College
Shepherdstown, WV 25443

University of Charleston
Charleston, WV 25304

West Liberty State College
West Liberty, WV 26074

West Virginia State College
Institute, WV 25112

West Virginia University
Morgantown, WV 26506

West Virginia Wesleyan College
Buckhannon, WV 26201

Wisconsin

Carthage College
Kenosha, WI 53141

Marquette University
  Milwaukee, WI 53233

University of Wisconsin-Eau Claire
  Eau Claire, WI 54701

University of Wisconsin-Green Bay
  Green Bay, WI 54301

University of Wisconsin-La Crosse
  La Crosse, WI 54601

University of Wisconsin-Madison
  Madison, WI 53706

University of Wisconsin-Milwaukee
  Milwaukee, WI 53201

University of Wisconsin-Oshkosh
  Oshkosh, WI 54901

University of Wisconsin-River Falls
  River Falls, WI 54022

University of Wisconsin-Superior
  Superior, WI 54880

Wyoming

University of Wyoming
  Laramie, WY 82071

MASTER'S DEGREE

Alabama

Auburn University, Auburn
  Auburn University, AL 36849

University of Alabama, University
University, AL 35486

Arizona

University of Arizona
Tucson, AZ 85721

California

Armstrong University
Berkeley, CA 94704

California State University, Long Beach
Long Beach, CA 90840

California State University, Los Angeles
Los Angeles, CA 90032

California State University, Northridge
Northridge, CA 91330

Golden Gate University
San Francisco, CA 94105

John F. Kennedy University
Orinda, CA 94563

National University
San Diego, CA 92108

Northrop University
Inglewood, CA 90306

West Coast University, Los Angeles
Los Angeles, CA 90020

Colorado

University of Colorado, Boulder
Boulder, CO 80309

University of Colorado, Colorado Springs
  Colorado Springs, CO 80933

University of Colorado, Denver
  Denver, CO 80202

University of Denver
  Denver, CO 80208

Connecticut

University of Bridgeport
  Bridgeport, CT 06601

University of Hartford
  West Hartford, CT 06117

Western Connecticut State University
  Danbury, CT 06810

District of Columbia

American University
  Washington, DC 20016

George Washington University
  Washington, DC 20052

Southeastern University
  Washington, DC 20024

Florida

Florida State University
  Tallahassee, FL 32306

Jacksonville University
  Jacksonville, FL 32211

University of Florida
  Gainesville, FL 32611

Georgia

Atlanta University
  Atlanta, GA 30314

Georgia State University
  Atlanta, GA 30303

Mercer University, Atlanta
  Atlanta, GA 30341

Illinois

DePaul University
  Chicago, IL 60604

Northern Illinois University
  DeKalb, IL 60115

Northwestern University
  Evanston, IL 60201

University of Chicago
  Chicago, IL 60637

Kansas

Wichita State University
  Wichita, KS 67208

Kentucky

Eastern Kentucky University
  Richmond, KY 40475

Louisiana

Louisiana State University, Baton Rouge
Baton Rouge, LA 70803

Louisiana Tech University
Ruston, LA 71272

Maryland

Loyola College
Baltimore, MD 21210

University of Baltimore
Baltimore, MD 21201

Massachusetts

Babson College
Babson Park, MA 02157

Harvard University
Cambridge, MA 02138

Michigan

Central Michigan University
Mount Pleasant, MI 48859

Eastern Michigan University
Ypsilanti, MI 48197

Grand Valley State College
Allendale, MI 49401

Michigan State University
East Lansing, MI 48824

Wayne State University
Detroit, MI 48202

Western Michigan University
  Kalamazoo, MI 49008

Missouri

Avila College
  Kansas City, MO 64145

Clayton University
  Clayton, MO 63105

Rockhurst College
  Kansas City, MO 64110

Southeast Missouri State University
  Cape Girardeau, MO 63701

Washington University, St. Louis
  St. Louis, MO 63130

Webster University
  Webster Groves, MO 63119

New Hampshire

Plymouth State College of the University of New Hampshire
  Plymouth, NH 03264

New Jersey

Fairleigh Dickinson University, Florham-Madison
  Madison, NJ 07940

Fairleigh Dickinson University, Rutherford
  Rutherford, NJ 07070

Fairleigh Dickinson University, Teaneck-Hackensack
  Teaneck, NJ 07666

Montclair State College
  Upper Montclair, NJ 07043

Seton Hall University
  South Orange, NJ 07079

New Mexico

University of New Mexico, Albuquerque
  Albuquerque, NM 87131

New York

Baruch College
  New York, NY 10010

Cornell University
  Ithaca, NY 14853

C.W. Post College
  Greenvale, NY 11548

Hofstra University
  Hempstead, NY 11550

Iona College
  New Rochelle, NY 10801

Long Island University, Brooklyn Center
  Brooklyn, NY 11201

New York University
  New York, NY 10003

Pace University, New York
  New York, NY 10038

Pace University, Pleasantville/Briarcliff
  Pleasantville, NY 10570

Pace University, White Plains
  White Plains, NY 10603

St. John's University
  Jamaica, NY 11439

Syracuse University
  Syracuse, NY 13210

Wagner College
  Staten Island, NY 10301

Ohio

Case Western Reserve University
  Cleveland, OH 44106

Kent State University, Kent
  Kent, OH 44242

Miami University, Oxford
  Oxford, OH 45056

University of Akron
  Akron, OH 44325

University of Toledo
  Toledo, OH 43606

Wright State University, Dayton
  Dayton, OH 45435

Xavier University
  Cincinnati, OH 45207

Youngstown State University
  Youngstown, OH 44555

Oklahoma

Central State University
  Edmond, OK 73034

Oregon

University of Oregon, Eugene
  Eugene, OR 97403

Pennsylvania

La Salle University
  Philadelphia, PA 19141

St. Joseph's University
  Philadelphia, PA 19131

Temple University
  Philadelphia, PA 19122

University of Pennsylvania
  Philadelphia, PA 19104

University of Scranton
  Scranton, PA 18510

Tennessee

Memphis State University
  Memphis, TN 38152

Texas

Amber University
  Garland, TX 75041

North Texas State University
  Denton, TX 76203

Prairie View A & M University
  Prairie View, TX 77446

St. Mary's University of San Antonio
  San Antonio, TX 78284

Texas A & M University, College Station
  College Station, TX 77843

University of Texas, Arlington
Arlington, TX 76019

Utah

University of Utah
Salt Lake City, UT 84112

Virginia

CBN University
Virginia Beach, VA 23463

Washington

Eastern Washington University
Cheney, WA 99004

Wisconsin

University of Wisconsin-Madison
Madison, WI 53706

Wyoming

University of Wyoming
Laramie, WY 82071

DOCTORAL DEGREE

Alabama

University of Alabama, University
University, AL 35486

District of Columbia

George Washington University
Washington, DC 20052

Georgia

Georgia State University
Atlanta, GA 30303

Illinois

Northwestern University
Evanston, IL 60201

University of Chicago
Chicago, IL 60637

Louisiana

Louisiana Tech University
Ruston, LA 71272

Massachusetts

Harvard University
Cambridge, MA 02138

Michigan

Michigan State University
East Lansing, MI 48824

Missouri

Clayton University
Clayton, MO 63105

International Graduate School
  St. Louis, MO 63108

Washington University, St. Louis
  St. Louis, MO 63130

New York

Cornell University
  Ithaca, NY 14853

New York University
  New York, NY 10003

Syracuse University
  Syracuse, NY 13210

Ohio

Case Western Reserve University
  Cleveland, OH 44106

Kent State University, Kent
  Kent, OH 44242

Oregon

University of Oregon, Eugene
  Eugene, OR 97403

Pennsylvania

Temple University
  Philadelphia, PA 19122

University of Pennsylvania
  Philadelphia, PA 19104

Texas

North Texas State University
  Denton, TX 76203

Texas A & M University, College Station
  College Station, TX 77843

University of Houston, University Park
  Houston, TX 77004

University of Texas, Austin
  Austin, TX 78712

Virginia

Virginia Commonwealth University
  Richmond, VA 23284